Going

Global

# Going Global

## How Europe Helps Small Firms Export

*William E. Nothdurft*

A German Marshall Fund of
the United States Book

The Brookings Institution
*Washington, D.C.*

Copyright © 1992

THE GERMAN MARSHALL FUND OF THE UNITED STATES

11 Dupont Circle, N.W., Washington, D.C. 20036


*Library of Congress Cataloging-in-Publication data*

Nothdurft, William E.
    Going global : how Europe helps small firms export / William E.
Nothdurft.
        p.    cm.
    Includes bibliographical references and index.
    ISBN 0-8157-6204-6 (alk. paper) : — ISBN 0-8157-6203-8
(pbk. : alk. paper)
    1. Foreign trade promotion—Europe.   2. Small business—
Government policy—Europe.   I. Title.
HF 1531.N65   1992                                    92-22243
382'.63—dc20                                              CIP


9 8 7 6 5 4 3 2 1


The paper used in this publication meets the minimum requirements of
the American National Standard for Information Sciences—Permanence of
paper for Printed Library Materials, ANSI Z39.48-1984

# Author's Acknowledgments

The crafting of any book is an effort to which many contribute. This book is no exception. I am deeply indebted to Anne Heald of the German Marshall Fund of the United States and David Geddes of the U.S. Department of Commerce's Economic Development Administration for their patience, encouragement, and support for the research on which this book is based. The findings and recommendations are mine, however, and do not necessarily reflect the views of either the Economic Development Administration or the German Marshall Fund.

I owe a great deal to the many public and private sector officials in Sweden, Denmark, Germany, France, Italy, and the United Kingdom who were not only generous with their time but extraordinarily candid about the strengths and weaknesses of the export assistance programs they administer. To the many individuals who reviewed the first draft of the manuscript, I also extend my thanks.

Finally, to Robert E. Friedman, chairman of the Corporation for Enterprise Development, who accompanied me during two study tours in Europe and provided his typically insightful analysis of the lessons we learned there, I offer my warmest thanks for his substantive contributions and for his friendship for nearly a decade.

# Contents

# Chapter 1

# Europe's Export Challenge

*Just downriver from London's financial district, where the River Thames loops around a seedy section of the city's East End known as the Isle of Dogs, one of the world's great trading centers is being reborn.*

*The Isle is part of "the Docklands," a maze of dilapidated wharves enclosing some seven hundred acres of protected water—once the largest port complex in the world. Here, in the Middle Ages, the Hanseatic League and the other European merchant guilds made London Europe's leading trading center. Here too, centuries later, the British East India Company and countless other traders bought and sold goods throughout the British Empire. In time, however, with the collapse of the empire, the Blitz, and fundamental shifts in the modes and patterns of trade, the ships and the merchants departed. By the 1980s, the area had become a wasteland, a desolate expanse of rotting piers and rusting cranes.*

*Today, however, in what is being called the largest redevelopment project in the world, the Docklands are being resurrected as an international trade and finance center. Construction cranes have replaced loading cranes, and the maritime hubbub of the docks has been replaced by the din of an international airport from which a new generation of merchants commutes to the trading capitals of a soon-to-be integrated European market, and beyond. A wide array of internationally oriented small- and medium-sized service and manufacturing businesses[1] occupies renovated warehouses and sleek new office buildings. And, in a move as symbolic as it is practical, the government agency that provides export credit guarantees to these and other British exporters has relocated to the Docklands. Once again the hub of a global trading network, the Isle of Dogs is back in business.*

This same aggressive internationalization is underway in Old World trading centers throughout Europe. The globalization

1

of markets in general, and the prospect of a Single European Market by the end of 1992 in particular, have heightened European attention to the export challenge and spawned an intriguing array of export assistance services designed to help even the smallest businesses become global competitors. Some of these initiatives are new and relatively untested; others are well established. The most interesting among them deal with exporting not as an end in itself but as part of a package of trade development initiatives. In the struggle to become more internationally competitive and to increase exporting among its small- and medium-sized businesses, the United States has much to learn from its European trading partners.

## Europe's Exporting Commitment

> You can no longer rely on your home market, because your home market is now an export market—for everybody else.
> *Niels Christian Nielsen, Danish Technology Institute*

The history of Europe is, among other things, a history of international market acquisition. With modest natural endowments and small domestic economies—at least compared with the United States—the nation-states of Europe historically have had little choice but to look outward. From the Age of Exploration to the Age of Empire and right up to World War II, the economies of Europe grew principally by acquiring territory and, in the process, gaining resources and captive markets for finished goods. More recently, however, the Europeans have evolved a more subtle strategy, one that replaces the acquisition of geography through conquest with the acquisition of niche markets through export trade. The game is the same, but the weapons are more sophisticated.

Europe's export intensiveness is dramatic. In 1989 exports represented half to two-thirds of gross national product (GNP) in Belgium, the Netherlands, and Ireland; from a quarter to nearly a third of GNP in Norway, Sweden, Denmark, Ger-

Table 1-1. *Export Intensity in Western Europe and the United States*

| Nation | 1989 exports as percent of 1989 gross national product | Nation | 1989 exports as percent of 1989 gross national product |
|---|---|---|---|
| Ireland | 69.9 | Portugal | 27.5[a] |
| Belgium | 64.4 | Austria | 25.8 |
| Netherlands | 48.3 | Finland | 20.1[b] |
| Norway | 30.4 | France | 18.7[b] |
| Germany | 28.3 | United Kingdom | 18.3 |
| Iceland | 28.1 | Italy | 16.4 |
| Sweden | 27.7 | Greece | 14.1 |
| Switzerland | 27.6 | Spain | 11.7 |
| Denmark | 27.6 | United States | 6.9 |

Source; Data derived from International Monetary Fund, *International Financial Statistics, April 1991* (Washington, 1991).

a. 1988 data
b. Percent of gross domestic product.

many, Switzerland, Austria, and Portugal; and between 10 and 20 percent of GNP in France, Italy, the United Kingdom, Finland, Greece, and Spain (see table 1-1). For the twelve-nation European Community as a whole, exports averaged more than 30 percent of total GNP. In contrast, U.S. exports were less than 7 percent of GNP. Germany, whose exports have nearly equaled U.S. exports in value for several years, is four times as export intensive as the United States.[2]

What accounts for such high export intensity? The simplest answer is necessity. The domestic markets of all but a few of these nations are simply too small to offer businesses much room for growth. Consequently, they trade with each other and with the world far more than does the United States. But this export intensity is also driven by a coherent trade strategy: these countries have recognized that the more the economy globalizes—and the more the economy of Europe becomes integrated after 1992—the more crowded their domestic economies will become. Thus, for most European nations, exporting isn't simply good economic policy; it is a matter of economic survival. Thomas Niles, former U.S. repre-

Table 1-2. *Export Promotion Spending of Seven Western Countries*

Millions of U.S. dollars

| Countries | Per capita | Per $1,000 of GNP/GDP | Per $1,000 federal spending |
|---|---|---|---|
| France | 6.19 | 0.47 | 1.95 |
| Germany | 1.67 | 0.11 | 0.68 |
| Italy | 3.74 | 0.29 | 0.64 |
| Sweden | 8.72 | 0.46 | 1.33 |
| United Kingdom | 2.85 | 0.28 | 1.24 |
| Canada | 21.44 | 1.48 | 6.02 |
| United States | 1.20 | 0.06 | 0.29 |

Source: U.S. Department of Commerce, "Export Promotion Activities of Major Competitor Nations," Washington, July 1988, p. 6.

sentative to the European Community, has noted, "Their entire economy is organized for exporting."[3]

So are their budget priorities. Among its major trading partners, the United States ranks last in export promotion spending related to total GNP or to total federal budgetary expenditures, even when agricultural trade promotion is included (see table 1-2).[4] In 1987, for example, the United States spent only $0.06 per $1,000 of its total GNP on export promotion, only $0.29 per $1,000 of total government spending, and only $1.20 per capita. America's closest major trading partner, Canada, spent twenty-five times as much as the United States in relation to GNP. Germany, although second-to-last in per capita spending on export promotion, nonetheless spent twice as much as the United States in relation to GNP or total federal expenditures.[5] Moreover, Germany's governmental spending on trade promotion activities merely augments a sophisticated and well-financed private sector promotional system; the United States has no comparable system.

In testimony before Congress, J. Michael Farren, U.S. Commerce Department undersecretary for international trade, presented graphic illustrations of the competitive disadvantage at which these investment levels place the United States: "In the fast-developing markets of Europe resulting from the EC 1992 process, the United States has three officers in Milan; the

French thirty-eight. Major export opportunities have arisen from the U.S.-Canada Free Trade Agreement. We have 8 officers in Canada; there are 112 Canadian commercial officers stationed in the United States. We are consistently out-staffed by major trade competitors."[6]

## Good News and Bad News: The U.S. Export "Turnaround"

> Exports are running solid and strong.
> *George Bush, 1991 State of the Union Address*

Compared with Europe, the United States, with its huge domestic market, has never had to concentrate much on active exporting. Historically, all but the largest American corporations have found plenty of room to grow at home. Often, exporting was what firms did to dump excess inventory when production temporarily overshot domestic demand—an on-again, off-again pattern that has been a source of friction with customers and trading partners alike. But after the recession of the early 1980s, this easy formula changed. While domestic customers vanished as America's industrial economy restructured, American firms found few overseas buyers to take up the slack because a soaring dollar made U.S. products prohibitively expensive. By 1987 America's merchandise trade deficit had reached a whopping $159 billion.[7]

Toward the end of the decade, however, after the over-valuation of the dollar had been corrected, U.S. export performance began to improve. Between 1987 and 1989, exports of goods and services expanded at an average annual rate of more than 14 percent, while imports grew only half as fast.[8] By 1991 the nation's trade deficit had narrowed to a few billion dollars, and U.S. Commerce Department Secretary Robert Mosbacher declared, "We are back producing high quality products, with exports continuing to provide strong support for economic activity in the United States."[9]

Has the United States finally turned the corner on trade?

Have American firms become global competitors again? The answer, for the most part, is no. The trade deficit shrank in late 1990 and early 1991, largely because American consumer demand for imports was in a recession-driven slump and imported oil was cheaper. As the value of U.S. imports dropped, exports looked better by comparison and the monthly trade deficit narrowed. Massive payments related to the Gulf War made by Saudi Arabia and Japan pushed the current account into surplus but had nothing to do with trade.

Across a fairly wide spectrum of industries, exports were growing as the 1990s began.[10] But a key reason for this development was that American products were cheaper than they had been in years. By February 1991 the dollar was worth roughly 30 percent less than it had been in February 1985.[11] In effect, every product American companies sold in the global marketplace was on sale at one-third off. And because, for the first time in recent memory, the economies of our major trading partners were booming while the U.S. economy lagged, American producers were able to find overseas customers who not only wanted to buy but had the means to take advantage of the bargains as well.

But it was a brittle boomlet; by the middle of 1991, a softening of the economies of America's major trading partners and a gradually strengthening dollar had begun to reduce overseas demand for U.S. products, though exports to Europe were still strong. Bargain days were over.

As for American competitiveness, the jury is still out. Certainly some firms—Motorola, General Electric, Xerox, and Boeing, among others—are fierce global competitors, cutting production costs and increasing product quality. But most American businesses, especially the bulk of the small- and medium-sized manufacturing firms that form the foundation of America's industrial capacity, have yet to retool, retrain, and reorient themselves to the tough new realities of the global marketplace—even though many are losing market share every day to competitors from Europe and elsewhere.[12]

## U.S. Export Patterns and the Role of Small Firms

American small firms do not think exporting because they are not hungry enough.
*Dr. Armin Grünewald, German Association of Chambers of Commerce and Industry*

The National Federation of Independent Business regularly asks its membership to rank seventy-five key business issues. In the latest survey, businesses ranked exporting last. It isn't an issue because they don't do it.

They are not alone. Despite steadily increasing international competition, few American companies export. According to C. Fred Bergsten, director of the Institute for International Economics, 15 percent of U.S. firms account for 85 percent of all American exports, and half of these companies are active in only one market. Only 20 percent of all U.S. exporters—3 percent of all U.S. businesses—sell in more than five countries abroad. [13] The Census Bureau estimates that just sixty-six firms account for 54 percent of all U.S. exports. [14]

Understanding with any precision how much U.S. firms export is difficult because of the shortage of reliable data. According to the Census Bureau's most recent enterprise statistics, just under 3.9 million enterprises employed workers in the United States in 1987, and only 104,564 of these firms— less than 2.7 percent of the total—reported any export activity. [15] In turn, these 104,564 enterprises operated some 546,000 individual establishments across the country, but fewer than 130,000 of those establishments (employing 10.3 million workers) engaged in export activity.

Late in 1991, the Foreign Trade Division of the Census Bureau matched the 1987 Enterprise Statistics and the shipper's export declarations (SEDs) filed by firms making export shipments. It was not an easy task: more than 40 percent of the SEDs filed in 1987 had incorrect, invalid, or unreported employer identification numbers.

   Despite these limitations, the new data present a revealing
picture of American export patterns. Some 71,000 enterprises
(manufacturers, wholesalers, and others) filed SEDs for export
shipments totaling $142 billion in 1987. Manufacturers repre-
sented only 40 percent of the firms reporting export activity,
but they accounted for nearly 75 percent of the total value
of SED-matched exports in 1987 and employed nearly 85
percent of the workers involved in export activity.[16] Shipments
of the SED-matched exporters ranged from a few thousand
dollars to more than $100 million. However, 55,000 of these
enterprises, or some 78 percent, had total shipments worth
less than $250,000; and almost 90 percent of these 55,000
firms made fewer than twelve shipments.[17] According to an
analysis of the SED data by *The Exporter* magazine, these
exporters averaged only six shipments a year at an average value
of only $7,800 per shipment. While these firms represented
78 percent of all exporting firms, they accounted for only 2
percent of the total value of all U.S. exports. In contrast, nearly
60 percent of the total value of all U.S. exports in 1987 was
shipped by a mere 0.2 of 1 percent of all exporting firms—the
largest ones.[18] In short, of the less than 3 percent of U.S. firms
that do export, most ship so little, and their shipments have
so little value, that they have little effect on the nation's balance
of trade.
   These figures have important implications for U.S. export
promoters in both the public and private sectors because they
make several things clear. First, what matters in exporting in
terms of jobs and the balance of trade is manufacturing. Second,
there is enormous room for export growth not only among the
tens of thousands of small-and medium-sized firms (SMEs) that
already export, but also among the hundreds of thousands of
nonexporting enterprises that have yet to explore export markets. According to Leslie Stroh, editor and publisher of *The
Exporter* magazine, "There is an almost perfect correlation
between the frequency of exports and the size of the exporter.
These infrequent exporters are small businesses. There is real
potential for significant export growth in these firms, but to

get that growth they'll need real help, not pep talks."[19] Pep talks, however, have long been the leading form of export assistance available to smaller firms in the United States. As recently as 1992, the federal government's most visible export promotion program was the National Export Initiative—a road show that had Commerce Department and other federal officials traveling from city to city to encourage firms to export, as if lack of enthusiasm were the principal barrier to increased SME exporting. Their audiences appear to have been unconvinced; of the 7,000 firms that participated in the conferences, only 350 subsequently returned for more detailed export assistance at a U.S. Department of Commerce district office.[20]

## Strategic Export Assistance: Learning from Europe

> The fundamental requirement is the adoption of a new mindset of export orientation by U.S. industry and government—for both the immediate future and the long term. Such attitudes are second nature in virtually all other countries.
>
> C. Fred Bergsten, Institute for International Economics

The federal government, most trade associations and chambers of commerce, and many states have been slow to recognize and respond to the mismatch between the needs of SMEs with export potential and the forms of export trade assistance typically available to them. Historically, the interests of large corporations, not SMEs, have predominated in the shaping of federal trade policy. The definition of "small business" used by the Commerce Department, the Export-Import Bank, and the Small Business Administration—a firm with fewer than 500 employees—is so all-encompassing that it covers all but 1 percent of U.S. manufacturers. Only 3,696 of the nation's 307,120 manufacturers have more than 500 employees, but nearly 90 percent have fewer than 50 employees.[21] The federal government acknowledges the special needs of SMEs but has found few ways to address them effectively.

In contrast, most European countries tend to pay closer attention to the needs of SMEs and provide tangible assistance for exporting and trade development.[22] Over the years, but especially during the past decade, the Europeans have developed export assistance programs that, in the best cases, are the result of a conscious attempt to find answers to five strategic questions about exporting and SMEs:

—Why don't more SMEs become regular and successful exporters?

—Which firms does it make sense to help?

—What forms of assistance are most effective for reaching and serving targeted firms?

—Who should deliver assistance; and where should it be delivered?

—How should it be delivered, and under what terms?

The chapters that follow address each of these strategic questions in turn and present ten practical lessons to be drawn from the experiences of some of the most innovative public and private SME export assistance service providers in six European nations: Germany, France, Italy, Britain, Sweden, and Denmark.

The central point, however, is that European countries provide—and, in some cases, have provided for years—a wide array of export assistance services designed to meet the special and individual needs of SMEs. The financial and political commitment to developing the export capabilities of small firms in these countries is impressive. The breadth and depth of the assistance available is substantial, from programs to help firms with their initial market explorations, to programs that network firms and in some cases actually broker individual transactions. Precisely who delivers this assistance (public agencies, private organizations, or public/private partnerships) varies widely. So does the locus of service delivery (nationally, regionally, locally). And an important caution is in order: some of these programs are new and relatively untested and even long-established programs are constantly being modified, abandoned, or reinvented. Consequently, definitive assessments of effectiveness are difficult. Nevertheless, the commitment these initiatives represent is powerful and remarkably uniform from country to country.

What matters in the pages that follow, therefore, is not the specific operating mechanics of the programs described, but the basic principles they embody and the widespread commitment they demonstrate to the development and maintenance of a private and public sector infrastructure for trade. Despite the differing political and economic circumstances of these nations, their initiatives offer lessons that are readily adaptable to the United States—lessons we would be wise to consider.

*Chapter 2*

# Why Most Small- and Medium-Sized Firms Don't Export

*Luciano Galletti leans back in his sleek black leather chair and looks out across the red tile roofs of Parma. Beyond the window stretches a crowded landscape of stone, brick, and cement-stucco buildings washed in the earth tones typical of northern Italy—ocher, burnt sienna, umber, and sage green. It is an ageless landscape in a muted palette, sprawling beneath a sky dulled by the gray pall of fog and auto exhaust hanging over the city. Italy in winter, colors by Armani.*

*Yet it is a scene that throbs with economic life. The streets are clogged with delivery trucks. Small industrial and commercial enterprises are wedged in everywhere—next to graceless Euro-modern apartment blocks, among simple stone houses that could date from the Renaissance, around the crisp green edges of a few incongruous fields. Housed in these hundreds of tiny workshops are many of Galletti's clients—the highly skilled artisans who have made northern Italy one of the most advanced manufacturing centers in the world. Galletti's organization, RESFOR, is a service center for these small firms, helping them to become indirect exporters by finding and screening large manufacturers, in Europe and elsewhere, that may provide subcontract work.*

*"We can bring the markets to them; this is not a problem," Galletti explains, turning back to his ultramodern office. "The problem is their small capacity to plan for the future. To make them exporters, we must first enter their mentality. Only then can we open their minds."*

## Understanding the Export Aversion of Small Firms

To the extent that a strategy guides state, federal, and private sector export assistance programs in the United States, it is the belief that if small- and medium-sized enterprises (SMEs) can be made aware of the opportunities exporting presents and

12

learn how to take advantage of those opportunities, they will become exporters. In 1984, for example, the U.S. House Small Business Committee's Subcommittee on Export Opportunities asserted that the chief barrier to exporting for small firms was a lack of information on export opportunities.[1]

But the comforting suggestion that the principal reason more SMEs in the United States don't export is because they are unaware of the opportunities exporting presents is naive. Certainly in the past, most U.S. manufacturers, with a domestic market more than adequate to meet their needs, have been myopic about international opportunities. And the evidence that many firms, especially small ones, still feel that way is persuasive.

But in the 1990s most business owners are at least aware of the challenge of international competition. Their trade papers are replete with stories about the global challenge, and, more important, their markets offer ample evidence of increasing competition. They understand, even if they have no coherent strategy to address the problem, that, as the authors of a recent book on international trade promotion noted, "Today the individual firm no longer has a choice about going international; remaining domestic may mean lost opportunities and even competition in its own backyard."[2]

So if awareness is not the key issue keeping many American SMEs from exporting as vigorously as their European counterparts, what is? Here are some clues:

—A survey by the research firm Yankelovich, Skelly, and White, commissioned by the Missouri Department of Commerce, found that one-third of small firms did not even consider exporting, despite the availability of state and federal assistance.[3]

—Another survey, conducted by the Small Business Association of New England, found that 75 percent of nonexporting firms do not attend export awareness or training seminars, though they apparently know about them.[4]

—A 1985 survey of 7,500 firms, conducted by the National Federation of Independent Business, found that nonexporters had very clear and pragmatic reasons for not exporting, including difficulty obtaining financing and market data and meeting product standards. Lack of awareness was not one of them.[5]

Discussion of export barriers in trade magazines, state houses, and congressional committees invariably, almost reflexively, turns to the lack of export finance vehicles as the principal barrier to SME exporting. But other barriers are even more fundamental. In one of the most thoughtful assessments to date of the policy implications of the export behavior of SMEs, Michigan State University researcher S. Tamer Cavusgil concluded, "Many U.S. firms are reluctant to consider export prospects and voluntarily exclude themselves from entering new markets because they perceive exporting as too risky, complicated, and not profitable. Others are simply indifferent to exporting and not willing to invest management time and money."[6] Distinguishing the real barriers to exporting from the assumed ones is crucial to the creation of effective export market development programs.

**Lesson 1:**   *The primary barriers to SME exporting are internal to firms, not external in markets.*

> The key is willingness; firms have to want to export.
> *Dr. Sergio Alessandrini, Bocconi University, Milan*

> We are networked around the world, but it is hard to get small companies to come around the corner to us.
> *Victor Vogt, Cologne Chamber of Commerce and Industry*

There are dozens of barriers to exporting, from problems as basic as language differences and export finance to those as byzantine as customs regulations and product standards. Their impressive export statistics suggest that most European countries have found ways of breaking down these barriers. Yet the directors of even the most successful European export assistance programs are frustrated with the difficulty of helping SMEs to export. At both the national and the European Community level, studies have been undertaken to get at the root of SME resistance to exporting. And while they confirm that there is no shortage of barriers to SME exporting, these studies—and the practical experience of those responsible for helping small firms export—point to one paramount problem: most SMEs don't export because their owner-managers have neither the time nor the inclination to think about it, not because the firms don't know they should.

In 1987 the British Overseas Trade Board (BOTB) commissioned an analysis of the export potential of the nation's SMEs (defined as companies with $2 million to $20 million in annual turnover). The study found that active SME exporters— firms that had exported more than 15 percent of turnover in at least one of the past three years— accounted for some 9 percent of total U.K.-manufactured exports. And in results that underscore the untapped potential of America's own infrequent exporters, the study also found that if passive exporters—firms that exported less than 15 percent of turnover—increased their export activity to the level of active exporters, Britain's foreign exchange earnings would be increased by more than $10 billion annually. What kept these firms from performing as well as the active exporters, the study discovered, was not external obstacles or organizational differences, but differences in attitudes among owner-managers. The BOTB study found that

—Active exporters dismissed procedural problems such as customs declarations and export documentation as minor inconveniences, while passive exporters and nonexporters saw them as important barriers;

—Passive and nonexporters perceived financing as a major barrier, but active exporters had little difficulty acquiring financing;

—Passive and nonexporters were apprehensive about language barriers, but active exporters did not think language differences were significant obstacles;

—Active exporters were twice as likely to have begun exporting in their first five years of existence and were twice as likely to be operating with a long-term plan than passive exporters;

—Among nonexporters, past export failure was not the cause of their lack of export activity; nearly three-quarters had never tried at all.

The British study concluded, "The most serious barriers to success in export markets . . . were not so much lack of competence as lack of knowledge, commitment, and persistence within the firms themselves."[7]

Penetrating an export market is a resource-intensive activity, requiring money to research the market, modify products, and finance deals; skilled people to develop, execute, and service those deals; and time to overcome a seemingly endless stream of procedural barriers. But the most important and scarcest resource required for successful exporting is the ability of the company's management to see beyond short-term barriers to the long-term benefits of exporting: earnings growth, longer production runs, product development, and market-risk-spreading, among others. In small firms where the owner-manager is preoccupied with the day-to-day responsibilities of simply keeping the business going, looking beyond the horizon may seem like a luxury.

In most SMEs, the export manager, research manager, marketing manager, shipping manager, finance manager, and personnel manager are all likely to be the same individual: the owner. Not surprisingly, a recent European Commission study of barriers to SME exporting found that exporters with little experience listed "no executive time" as their most important problem.[8] Under these conditions, the fact that firms seldom have a coherent export market development strategy is even less surprising. And the more successful a small business is in its home market, the less time its owner is likely to have to explore export markets.

Consequently, many firms that try exporting begin haphazardly, responding to a chance order from overseas or to an isolated offer for overseas representation without thinking carefully about the long-term effects on the company. In a study funded by the British Department of Trade and Industry, Martin Parnell of the Liverpool Business School found that only a minority of SME exporters have a coherent strategic plan for export market development.[9]

### Lesson 2: *Export development is part of company development; it is a process, not an event.*

> Exporting is just one part of a web of company development issues—quality, flexibility, training—and cannot be separated from them.
> *Poul Breum, International Company Development, Danish Technology Institute*

> Simply crossing a border is not the issue. The issue is the strategic development of the company overall; eventually, that will lead to exports.
> *Bjorn Osterlind, Swedish National Industrial Board*

In 1987 the American Business Conference, an organization of some of the nation's most successful midmarket firms, commissioned a study to examine the international trade experiences of its members. Among other things, the study found that many of the most successful companies had gone global early in their lives. Says John Endean, ABC's vice president for policy, "We learned that exporting has less to do with how old a company is or how deep its pockets are than it does with managerial vision about market positioning. Good companies integrate exporting into the heart of their corporate plan right from the start."[10]

Even as they point proudly to their export trade figures, European export assistance program managers, public and private sector alike, caution that few firms think strategically about exporting from the beginning. According to Adele Massi, external affairs officer for Italy's principal export promotion agency, the Institute for Foreign Trade, "The problem is that there are too many 'adventurers'—companies with no strategy at all—who get into exporting one year and fall out the next."[11] Michele Simonin, research director for the Paris Chamber of Commerce and Industry, echoes Massi's point: "Most French companies export 'improvisationally'—shipping 6 or 8 percent of production abroad one year, then nothing the next."[12] According to Gunter Kayser of the Institute for Research on Medium-Sized Firms, even in Germany "Most exports are the result of an accidental foreign order, not a company strategy."[13]

The cost of these adventures can be high. One study of companies that fail at exporting indicates that they are twice as likely to have responded to an unsolicited order than to have developed a specific export plan.[14] Göran Sjöberg, director of the Swedish Trade Council's innovative Export Manager-for-Hire program (see chapter 3), suggests that companies must address three key issues before they branch off into exporting:

—Export Maturity. Many companies begin exporting before they have a solid management base, reliable products, sufficient sales experience, or adequate financial resources.

—Market Choice. Many companies let markets choose them through unsolicited orders rather than determining for themselves whether a given market demands their product, offers the best prices, or provides a compatible business culture.

—Export Vehicle Choice. Many companies are lured into binding relationships with distributors or sales representatives without exploring other options, including branch operations, subsidiaries, joint ventures, indirect exporting through inter-mediaries, or simply other distributors and representatives. In any situation, the choice of an export vehicle depends on the company, product, and market.[15]

Kent Goldmann, one of Sjöberg's roving export managers, advises, "The key is to concentrate strategically on a few markets with the right fit and the right agents and turn away all the others."[16]

This is easier said than done. Few firms take the trouble to scrutinize a new export order to consider its long-term implications. If the domestic market is strong and production capacity is fully utilized, most firms will ignore or decline the order. If the domestic market is in a slump and production capacity is underutilized or inventory is piling up, some firms will try to fill the order. But they will take the easiest route—presuming they can obtain financing—without giving much thought to the financial and strategic implications of committing themselves to the specific market or agent. Depending on the nature of the deal and the cost of the financing, this improvisational exporting can deplete exporters' resources and even place their future in jeopardy. As Stefan Wengler of the Federation of German Industries explains, "So long as they are successful in their markets they see no reason to go overseas; if they wait until domestic markets slip, they will not have the financial strength to export."[17]

To overcome adventurism and help firms think strategically about their export options, the Europeans have tried several techniques. Some attempt to build export expertise in firms through management training. Others take an active role in brokering individual deals. And still others have third-party organizations provide export expertise (see chapter 3). One Danish program, however, helps firms rethink their corporate plans in order to make exporting successful from the beginning.

### PROGRAM PROFILE
*Strategic Exporting—Denmark's International Company Development Project*

With an economy dominated by small firms whose survival depends on export growth, Denmark has recently embarked on a comprehensive program to upgrade the technical and managerial sophistication of even the smallest firms and establish them among Europe's most skilled exporters. One component of this effort (others are described elsewhere) is the International Company Development Program operated by the Danish Technology Institute, one of Europe's premier research and technology deployment centers.

According to Poul Breum, senior consultant for enterprise

management at the institute, two barriers stand in the way of internationalizing more small Danish firms. The first is the tendency, on the occasions when these firms do export, to deal only with Denmark's traditional trading partners, the United Kingdom and Scandinavia. The second and more difficult is getting the managers of otherwise sophisticated firms to think strategically for the first time.[18]

To address these problems, the Danish Technology Institute, in cooperation with the Irish Productivity Center and the Dutch Institute for Small and Medium Craft Businesses, designed a program not simply to promote exporting among SMEs, but to use the challenge posed by the coming integration of the European Community as a mechanism for helping a limited number of firms to develop new corporate plans with exporting as a major component.

"Making an export does not make you international," Breum explains. "Export development has to be part of a company strategy for growth; if not, you fail in the end." With funding from the EC Social Fund, the governments of Denmark, Ireland, and the Netherlands, and participating firms from each country, the three institutes identified enterprises with fifty employees or more, sufficient domestic market strength to be stable, management developed into well-defined divisions, and a desire to internationalize. Eighteen companies were chosen for the pilot program, six from each country.

During the eighteen-month program, management teams from each firm attended six national seminars on general management, export marketing management, financial controls management, technology and production management, leadership and organization culture, and strategic management and planning. They also participated in three international seminars on export marketing, technology and production, and leadership and organization. Each seminar required significant additional work by the management teams, and facilitators visited the companies regularly. The program's main product is a comprehensive two- to five-year rolling plan for internationalizing each firm. A secondary product is the creation within and between the three countries of trade networks of trained and motivated smaller firms capable of influencing, by design or example, the behavior of other firms in their sector or region. According to the organizers, nearly all the participating firms have successfully implemented their internationalization plans. The Danish Technology Institute, in the meantime, has expanded the program to several other EC countries, including Spain, Portugal, Italy, France, and the U.K. Plans are underway to expand into Eastern Europe as well.

What the companies learn from the program, besides the management techniques required to succeed in international markets, according to Breum, is "that a different culture is not so big a barrier, a different language is not so big a barrier, and being small is not so big a barrier. The big barrier is within your own company."[19]

*Chapter 3*

# Who Should Be Helped to Export

*Filkins is the quintessential English village: tucked away in the patchwork folds of the countryside, ancient cottages built of mellow limestone the color of aged cheddar cluster around the junction of two narrow country lanes. Ivory-pink roses ramble over lichen-encrusted stone walls. There are a venerable parish church and a welcoming pub. At the edge of the village is a massive stone barn, recently restored. A small black-and-white sign outside announces, quietly, that the barn is the home of "Cotswold Woolen Weavers."*

*Inside, Richard Martin presides over what appear to be the last vestiges of the Industrial Revolution: a throbbing, clanking, clattering collection of machines that look to have been manufactured well before Victoria became queen, all noisily carding, spinning, and weaving wool into blankets, shawls, and yard goods for suits and dresses.*

*But appearances are deceiving. In fact, despite the ancient looms—or perhaps because of them—Cotswold Woolen Weavers is able to produce fine fabrics to global standards of quality on short, flexible production runs that permit it to custom weave products to the specifications of its wholesale customers. As for exporting, "Oh yes," Martin shouts above the din. "We've been exporting almost from the beginning. Probably 80 percent of our turnover is exported."*

## Lesson 3: *Target assistance to the export ready.*

We have learned that the size of the firm is not what matters; what matters is the mentality of the firm—its readiness.
*Enrico Ricotta, Strategie & Accordi S.r.l., Rome*

We don't help just anyone, we examine their export planning sophistication.
*Johannes Olesen Larsen, Danish National Agency for Industry and Trade*

22

Export assistance programs in Europe, whether operated by public or private sector entities, target small- and medium-sized enterprises (SMEs), just as in the United States. Although the definitions of small and medium vary from country to country, and even from region to region *within* countries, the reasons for trying to reach SMEs are the same. First, there are a lot of these firms, many have export potential, and many already do some exporting. Second, unlike large firms, SMEs have fewer internal resources to use for exporting and typically cannot afford the high cost of privately provided export services. Third, the resources available to support assistance programs are too modest to be of much use to more than a handful of large firms and, in any event, such firms typically have well-developed export systems of their own.

Recently, however, even countries that have defined SMEs narrowly have concluded that, when it comes to export interest, capacity, and commitment, all SMEs are not created equal, and trying to treat them as though they were is fruitless. Throughout Europe, both public and private sector providers of export assistance and promotion services are shifting away from programs designed to encourage all SMEs to export and toward initiatives focused on export-ready firms with sufficient management capacity to develop and follow through on an export strategy.

This is a form of triage. Private and quasi-private sector export service providers, such as the German, French, or Italian chambers of commerce, for example, have limited their aid to motivated and well-prepared SMEs for some time. Now public sector export service providers have begun to follow suit. This shift is due only in part to the tight budgetary conditions facing all industrialized countries. It is also the result of experience. Working with firms that were not export ready simply was not producing results. Program managers have concluded that lavishing detailed technical assistance on a firm that is unprepared strategically not only wastes money but also threatens the stability of the firm itself. Consequently, in some countries, certain forms of assistance, such as market research or trade fair participation support, are now restricted to firms with an approved strategic plan for exporting. In addition, many formerly free services now require firms requesting help to prove their commitment in the form of a significant investment (see chapter 6).

Increasingly, significant export assistance is provided only to firms that have participated in an export audit designed both to illuminate the firm's capabilities and export readiness and to help company executives understand the issues associated with exporting.

### PROGRAM PROFILE
*Determining "Readiness" through Export Audits*

To improve the efficiency of public expenditures on export assistance to SMEs and reduce export adventurism, Britain, Germany, Sweden, France, and Denmark have all created formal export audit programs. The objective is to separate the export ready from the merely export willing. In most cases, these audits are part of a national strategy, though the assistance is delivered through both public and private regional or local organizations. Often these audit services are supplied not by government officials, but by private consultants whose fees are shared by the firms and the government.

The United Kingdom has moved to delegate much of the responsibility for providing market research services to local or regional branches of the Association of British Chambers of Commerce (ABCC) and a network of thirty-four export development advisors under contract to the ABCC. The initiative provides more than $4 million in "pump-priming" government funds over three years, but the chambers of commerce and their clients are responsible for picking up part of the cost after the first year. Government funding declines from 100 percent in the first year to 75 percent, 50 percent, and zero by the fourth year. As part of this process, the London Chamber of Commerce has created a free Confidential Export Audit program designed to ascertain the level of interested firms' commitment to exporting. "We want to be sure," one London Chamber executive explained, "that they see exporting as a natural development of their home base, not a cure for their home ills—that exporting is part of an integral business plan."[1] The audit covers financial details, products and services, stock levels, production capacity and limitations, R&D history, U.K. customers, sales, existing and potential competition, growth or contraction, and export experience, among other factors. If the audit shows the company to be export ready, a first-stage action plan can be developed at a cost of roughly $50 an hour to cover such items as markets, credit insurance, selling channels, customs requirements, payment, transport, documentation, trading terms, and foreign regulation.[2] Of the 120 initial participants in the program, 40 reported increased export earnings totaling nearly $8 million by the second year—from a program costing only $300,000.[3]

The German state of North Rhine-Westphalia offers a similar audit scheme, as the first stage in its export *Partner Search* program. Firms with an annual turnover of less than $10 million contact the Foreign Trade Institute, a joint venture of the chambers of commerce and craft and the state government, to apply for audit assistance. The institute provides private consultants for up to fifteen days and covers between 40 and 50 percent of cost, up to a maximum of roughly $13,000.[4] The consultant undertakes a comprehensive review of the firm, covering issues that include staffing, production capacity, existing markets and distribution networks, management structure and commitment, proposed markets, development and promotion budgets, and the form of overseas representation likely to best serve the firm's objectives. But in practice, according to institute officials, firms request this assistance when an export opportunity arises accidentally, not as a consequence of a strategic decision to begin exporting. Similar government-assisted export audit services are offered in several other German states, on slightly different terms.

In Sweden, the National Industrial Board (an agency of the Ministry of Industry) delivers export development and other development services to SMEs through a network of Regional Development Funds (RDFs), regional planning and development assistance agencies administered by county councils. A few years ago, the board undertook an export audit program called Export Pulse, which worked through the RDFs to help small firms with export potential develop their capacity through strategic development and market research. The program included an internal analysis by a consultant to the RDF; exploration of export opportunities in several markets to analyze size, structure of distribution channels, competition, price structures, and other factors; identification of target markets; and development of an export strategy for a specific market. The initial company assessment was fully funded by the government through the RDF, but market studies and strategy development planning were paid for largely by the firms themselves. Over several years, the program reached some 1,000 firms, and roughly 450 went on to export successfully to their targeted markets. Although the program was judged successful, it was designed only as a campaign that would run for a fixed period to generate local interest in export opportunities.

Until last year, Denmark had perhaps the most carefully structured SME export market development assistance system in Europe, one component of which was a Pre-Market Diagnosis program to determine the export-readiness of small firms with no previous export experience. Under the terms of this program, a firm could receive a soft loan from the National Agency of Industry and Trade (a division of the Ministry of Industry) to cover up to 70 percent of the cost of hiring a consultant to both determine its export readiness and develop an internal strategic plan covering not just exporting, but company structure and management, product development, and distribution systems, among other things. In fact, completing such a pre-market diagnosis was a prerequisite for approval of subsequent market development assistance (see chapter 4). If the company ultimately succeeded in penetrating the target market, the small pre-market loan had to be repaid; if not, the loan was forgiven. According to an agency official, one important benefit of this audit function was that "it persuaded many small companies not to go further and saved them a lot of money."[5]

## HOW SMALL IS "SMALL BUSINESS"?

In Europe, as in the United States, export assistance programs target SMEs. And, as in the United States, there is little agreement in Europe about what constitutes an SME. A recent European Commission study of SME export barriers hedged on an exact definition, creating three categories instead: small (20-49 workers), small medium (50-99), and large medium (100-500).[6] Any enterprise with fewer than twenty workers is typically called a microenterprise or artisan firm.

In most European export assistance programs, a firm's size is measured by either the number of workers or the annual turnover, and often both. Even within individual nations, the definition of small and medium may vary by subregion and assisting organization.

For example, in Denmark a major bank with a significant commitment to financing small business export transactions defines small as firms with 50 to 200 employees and an annual turnover of $7 million to $35 million. By Danish standards, however, these are fairly large firms. The Danish Ministry of Industry's recently restructured export assistance programs focused on firms with no more than $5 million in exports in any one market, and a new export-oriented networking program aims to make much smaller firms (five employees or more) internationally competitive.

In Sweden, the most common definition of an SME is any firm with fewer than 200 employees. However, most programs focus on much smaller firms—the 96 percent of Swedish firms with fewer than twenty employees.

In France, the organization chartered by the government to help small firms establish themselves in overseas markets defines small firms as those with fewer than 500 employees and

turnover under about $80 million—more medium large than
small. But the most successful regional programs focus on
much smaller firms, with $4 million to $20 million in annual
turnover.

As a matter of policy, Italy aims its export assistance programs at firms that have fewer than 500 employees and produce "high value added" and "innovative" products, but recent
research suggests that, in practice, many national programs
benefit more traditional industries that produce machinery, consumer durables, textiles, and agricultural products. The largest
beneficiaries of Italy's export assistance programs are firms with
more than 500 employees.[7]

In Germany, firms with fewer than 500 employees and an
annual turnover of under $50 million constitute 99.8 percent
of all businesses and form the backbone of the country's economy. Only 3,000 of Western Germany's 2 million enterprises
are larger. Given this dominance, SME economic policy is, in
effect, national economic policy: what's good for these firms,
called the *Mittelstand*, is good for Germany. And, as manag-
erment analyst Tom Peters has noted, these firms "eat, sleep,
and breathe export."[8] Yet even in Germany, export assistance
programs focus on small firms with low annual turnover. For
example, in North Rhine-Westphalia, one of the three most aggressive exporting states in Germany,[9] many export assistance
programs are limited to firms with less than $10 million in an-
nual turnover.

---

## Lesson 4: *Train the export willing—or create intermediary bodies to handle exporting for them.*

The main barrier to exporting for SMEs isn't resources,
it is knowledge of how to identify and secure export
opportunities.
*Göran Sjöberg, Swedish Trade Council*

Many more SMEs are export willing than are export ready. But
the knowledge and skill requirements for successful exporting

can be daunting. Firms must undertake market research, acquire live trade leads, identify and investigate overseas representatives, develop relationships with shippers and insurers, package products for overseas shipment, and meet customs requirements and product standards. Few SMEs have the capacity to address these issues competently even if they are motivated to begin exporting—a fact of life that may explain why the attrition rate for first-time exporters is as high as 50 percent, according to some studies.[10]

There are essentially two ways of helping companies that are interested in exporting but lack the internal skills necessary to do so successfully. The first, and most common, is to train company staff in the intricacies of export market development. The second is to have public, private, or quasi-private organizations act on the company's behalf—a growing trend in Europe, especially at the local and regional levels.

THE TRAINING OPTION. Like the United States, the Europeans have been providing export training for years. However, the similarity ends there. According to the most recent survey of the National Association of State Development Agencies, the fifty states, Puerto Rico, and the Virgin Islands held more than 1,500 international trade seminars in 1990. Most of these training seminars (many cosponsored by federal agencies and private organizations) tended to be general and largely motivational.[11] A recent review of state export assistance programs, conducted by the state of Michigan, noted that, "Export seminars, the tool most often used for skill development of sellers, have been poorly attended, and many would evaluate these sessions as worthless to most companies."[12] Michigan's conclusion was that export training must be tailored to the needs of individual companies to have any value.

Many European countries came to the same conclusion some years ago. Today, most export training in Europe is narrowly focused (on either specific industry sectors or markets, or both) and technical (addressing the nuts and bolts of export strategy development and techniques). In part, the difference in approach results from the difference in audience. As one recent comparative analysis noted, while the United States, and, to a lesser extent, the United Kingdom face "higher resistance levels among non-exporters," most European nations "find little need to persuade or motivate their firms to export."[13] Interviews with European export program managers suggest that the picture is not that simple, however. Frustrated by the fact that many SMEs display little interest in exporting, despite the prospect of massive new competition when the Single European Market arrives in 1993, many officials report that they have sharply reduced their motivational and general "how-to" seminars. While they may occasionally mount brief awareness campaigns, the bulk of their effort now goes to training the export willing in the fundamentals of becoming export ready.

Sweden is a good example. Its principal export promotion agency is the Swedish Trade Council, a publicly chartered but independent organization supported equally by the government and private industry. It has a staff of roughly 200 trade specialists in Stockholm (some sector specific, others market specific) and 200 more in embassies, consulates, and trade offices abroad. Its overseas trade commissioners are not foreign service personnel but staff recruited from industry for temporary tours of duty. The council, through its Institute of Export Training, offers export-willing SMEs a wide array of specific seminars, including courses in marketing and selling tailored to companies at different stages of export development. Company-tailored in-house training is also available, along with courses in international negotiation techniques, payment and financing, export procedures such as country-of-origin rules and customs, packaging, transportation, distribution, languages, and cultural studies. Finally, the institute offers a six-week international market development course for experienced export executives.

This pattern of narrowly targeted training is repeated throughout Europe. In Italy, the Institute for Foreign Trade (ICE), the principal export promotion agency, which reports to the Ministry of Foreign Trade, provides advanced training for export professionals, and the regional chambers of commerce provide seminars on exporting procedures and transactions. In Germany, the chamber of commerce and trade association systems, sometimes in cooperation with state governments, provide similar training. In France, the French Center for Foreign Commerce (CFCE), a government-chartered and supported corporation responsible for export information, promotion, and consultation, offers export-willing firms a wide range of seminars that focus primarily on specific opportunities in foreign markets or sectors. These seminars are offered both in Paris and through twenty-four regional offices and the regional chambers of commerce. CFCE derives nearly half of its variable costs budget from fees charged for these seminars and other services (see chapter 6).

But even these more carefully targeted training programs assume that a firm has the organizational capacity to undertake exporting—an assumption program officials agree may be too optimistic. Consequently, training for the export willing is becoming even more narrowly targeted and, increasingly, focuses on individual firms.


## PROGRAM PROFILE
*Sweden's Export Manager-for-Hire Program*

In Sweden, companies with sufficient internal capacity to mount export marketing drives can obtain the help of an export consultant to develop a strategic plan for penetrating a market, with the Swedish Trade Council covering part of the cost. The consultancy can run up to sixty hours, with the council picking up 60 percent of the tab.

But for firms that lack internal capacity to begin exporting (typically small producers with a domestic niche that seek to

expand beyond their home market), the council can provide an
export manager-for-hire—an export professional with substantial private sector experience, who works under contract to the
council. Under this scheme, companies hire 20 to 40 percent
of an export manager's time for two to four years. During this
time, the manager functions as the company's own export
director, helping management design an export plan, identifying potential markets, contacting potential customers, sug-
gesting product modifications, and so forth, while at the same
time training company personnel in export techniques. The
company bears 49 percent of the cost of the manager's services
in the first year (roughly $50 an hour), 75 percent in the second
year ($75 an hour), and 95 percent in the third ($95 an hour).
In the fourth year, a company can continue to use the manager's
services, but it must bear the full cost. In most cases, however,
firms are capable of managing on their own by year four.

In 1989 the Trade Council had twenty-three such export
managers, all but one located in central and southern Sweden,
where most of the country's industry is concentrated. Some
managers focus on a specific geographic region in Sweden and
can be accessed through the country's network RDFs, while
others specialize in specific industry sectors or overseas markets
and are headquartered in Stockholm. In either case, the managers also serve as channels of access to a wide range of Trade
Council business development services, banking and other
private sector services, and RDF-based local economic development services.

The export managers-for-hire do not provide training only
to new-to-export firms. According to Trade Council export
consultant Kent Goldmann, many of his clients are marginal
or failed exporters: "Sometimes their product isn't right for the
market, or the country they chose was not a good fit, or their
approach or agents are not right." But whether the client is
new to export or a marginal or failed exporter, Goldmann says,
the export manager-for-hire's job is the same—to eventually
become superfluous. Denmark and Norway have established
similar programs.

## PROGRAM PROFILE
*Denmark's Export Assistant Training Program*

Even small firms with committed and skilled owner-managers pursuing well-planned export strategies have export administration problems. For example, when the owner is overseas developing markets, there commonly is no one back home capable of taking overseas calls (sometimes in another language), handling orders, or overseeing shipments and documentation.

To increase export administration capacity in small firms, the local branch of Denmark's National Union of Clerks in Aarhus, working in cooperation with the Aarhus branch of the Federation of Danish Employers and the Aarhus School of Commerce, has developed an export assistant training curriculum. The objective is to create a cadre of young office workers fluent in another language, conversant with the technical vocabulary of exporting, knowledgeable in business organization and management, trained in the type of communication and information technologies essential to export trade (faxes, telexes, computer databases, business graphics, spreadsheets, and word processing), skilled in the procedural details of export transactions, and familiar with the cultural norms of other nations. The eighteen-month course alternates classroom study with two-month internships in small exporting firms and includes one month of intensive language study in the country that is the focus of the course.

Demand for the trainees, most of whom are unemployed when they begin, has been high. Of one group of twenty-two students, twelve had jobs in exporting within a week of completing the course. Of another group of seventeen trainees, thirteen quickly found work in exporting or importing, and the rest were offered ordinary office jobs. Since its inception in 1988, the program has expanded to include modular training packages aimed at the challenges and opportunities presented to European SMEs by the Single European Market.

The story behind the program's genesis is almost as intriguing as the program itself. "As it became clear that future wage growth would be limited," explains union official Jens Mastrup, "we decided we needed to deal with all the things our members value in their lives, not just wages and work conditions. Career training is one example, and we feel demand for it will only grow."[14]

THE EXPORT SERVICE ORGANIZATION OPTION. In their more candid moments, many European export program managers confess that SME owner-managers capable of producing high-quality products with significant export potential are often simply not equipped, either educationally or psychologically, to design, execute, and manage export market development programs on their own. Rather than trying to train these entrepreneurs in an area that may not interest them and for which they may have little talent, economic development officials in some parts of Europe (especially Italy and France) have begun to establish programs that identify, research, explore, and finally broker export agreements on behalf of the companies.

In some respects this is not a new idea. Private entrepreneurs—banks, major accounting firms, shipping companies, and freight forwarders, among others—have always been available for a fee to handle tasks involved in exporting for producers. But many, and possibly most, SMEs cannot afford the fees charged by such private service providers, and often the services themselves are quite limited. The oldest and newest private sector export service organizations—trading houses that date from the thirteenth century and trading companies that have emerged in the United States in the last decade—offer the most comprehensive services to would-be exporters. Oversimplifying somewhat, trading houses purchase goods from producers and market these goods wherever they command the best price. Export trading companies operating on a commission facilitate export deals. The main criticism of trading houses is that, while they relieve producers of inventory and headaches, they tend to pay the lowest possible price for goods they receive. Export trading companies handle smaller transactions, operate on fixed and narrow margins established by the seller and buyers in the marketplace, and survive by generating volume. The problem, as one expert has observed, is that when an export trading company is successful, it loses its client.[15] That is, after a company pays a few commission checks and its trade with a customer becomes regular, the trading company is cut out of the loop.

Partly in response to the limitations of such private intermediary institutions, and more importantly to the limitations of many SME owner-managers, hybrid organizations are emerging. The trend began in the Emilia-Romagna region of northern Italy. Twenty years ago, the economy of Emilia-Romagna, composed principally of small, family-owned industrial firms, lagged behind most other regions in Italy. In 1970, its per capita income was only 90 percent of the national average. Today, it is one of the nation's economic leaders. Its manufacturers are among the world's most advanced, and its per capita income is 120 percent of the national average. The history and mechanics of this renaissance are well documented in the recent literature on Italy's flexible manufacturing networks.[16] But one key element has been the creation by ERVET, the quasi-public economic development corporation created in 1974 to turn Emilia-Romagna's economy around, of a series of service centers designed to provide sophisticated business services to networks of manufacturing firms too small to afford them on their own. Some of these centers serve only one industrial sector, but others offer their expertise to all companies in the region. One such service center helps small firms become exporters by doing some of the work of export market development for them.

PROGRAM PROFILE
*Italy's SVEX*

The Service Center for the Export Development of Emilia-Romagna Firms, or SVEX, was created in 1989 jointly by ERVET, the regional chamber of commerce, and the production associations for small, medium, large, and artisan firms. SVEX was designed to solve two problems. First, the regional chamber of commerce, like many others, had long helped small firms participate in important trade fairs throughout Europe and elsewhere in the world. But once a fair was over and the firms returned to Italy, the chamber had no way to ensure that companies followed up on trade leads generated during the fair and thus no way to realize the benefits of sponsorship. Second, in a complaint about the weakness of national export promotion agencies echoed elsewhere in Europe, ERVET was frustrated by the inability of ICE to provide detailed service to individual firms or groups of firms.

According to Mauro Cavagnaro, the head of its marketing department, SVEX aims to establish long-term trade relationships in selected sectors between Emilia-Romagna firms and carefully targeted overseas markets where the organization perceives the region either has a competitive advantage or can take advantage of a political opportunity. Operating on the assumption that Italian firms need no help in penetrating European markets, SVEX researches untapped but potentially important difficult markets such as the former Soviet Union, India, and Japan. It conducts a detailed market analysis; finds an appropriate political, cultural, or trade event to promote the region's firms; organizes a group of firms interested in and capable of trading with the target country; invites officials from that country to visit the firms in Emilia-Romagna; and eventually establishes a permanent presence in that market, typically an overseas national under contract to SVEX. In addition to representing individual firms and groups of firms, SVEX is, in effect, a service center for service centers in the region's other sectors.

The essential service SVEX provides relieves the region's small firms of the tasks of identifying, researching, exploring, and gaining a foothold in new markets—activities which, because of their size, they are unlikely ever to undertake. SVEX accepts that some firms with exportable products may never be export ready and, by acting for them, helps them export in spite of themselves. SVEX's first-year budget of 500 million lire was funded by ERVET, but SVEX is expected to become self-supporting through fees charged to its customers.

*Chapter 4*

# What Forms of Export Assistance Work Best

*Brittany, France's wind-whipped, western-most province, is a place apart—not quite a part of France and, at first glance, not quite a part of this century. Its landscape has the quaint, timeless quality of its namesake, Britain: gently rolling, patchwork farmland with thatch-roofed farmhouses of pink or gray granite, crowded medieval market towns full of ancient, half-timbered buildings, and a battered coastline with busy fishing ports sheltered from the Atlantic gales by massive old stone jetties. Its native tongue, Breton, is Celtic, like Welsh or Gaelic, not French. And the people of Brittany cling to their language proudly as an emblem of their individuality.*

*Though isolated from the rest of France, Brittany has seldom been isolated from the rest of the world. Long before the Edict of Union joined it to France in 1532, the duchy had been an export trading center. Today that outward orientation continues. Major U.S. and Japanese corporations (Westinghouse, International Harvester, Carrier, and Canon, among others) have gained access to the emerging Single European Market by establishing subsidiaries in Brittany. But more important, in the last decade Brittany has created one of France's most dynamic regional economies, combining traditional strengths in fishing and agriculture with a strong R&D infrastructure that has helped spawn new biotechnology, electronics, telecommunications, and plastics industries, among others—all export oriented.*

*Christian Courvoisier's firm, EMO, with offices in a modern industrial park amid the artichoke fields west of Rennes, the region's commercial capital, embodies the new Brittany. Established less than a decade ago, EMO is already France's leading producer of sophisticated wastewater treatment equipment, with an annual turnover in excess of $7 million.[1] Only two years after its founding, the firm was exporting—first to nearby Belgium, then to Canada, the United Kingdom, Spain, Taiwan, and the United States. But EMO did not use France's many national*

*export assistance programs, which Courvoisier characterizes as "too*
*bureaucratic, too general." Instead, EMO turned to the local chamber*
*of commerce and to MIRCEB, a new regionally supported private*
*organization that helps Breton firms to export by researching new markets,*
*finding suitable joint venture partners, and negotiating agreements on a*
*partly subsidized, fee-for-service basis. "We needed to know very specific*
*things: the best geographic location in a foreign market, who is technically*
*and commercially qualified to be a partner, how reliable clients are and*
*what their real motivations are," Courvoisier explains. "The national*
*programs are not equipped to help us answer these questions."*

## Lesson 5:   *There are external barriers to SME exporting, but they are surmountable.*

SMEs do not have trouble adapting to export market
customs, just learning what those customs are.
*Dr. Angela Airoldi, Bocconi University, Milan*

Exporting is scary. Assuming that barriers such as language,
customs, standards, and procedures can be overcome and adequate representation found in alien markets, the financial
exposure alone can be crippling. Uncertainty is a given: the
slightest hiccup in the global political scene can kill a deal that
has been years in the making. The more unfamiliar the market,
the more uncertain the transaction and the more formidable
the barriers.

As a consequence, even in countries with a long history
of small- and medium-sized enterprise (SME) exporting, much
of the trade is between countries with strong natural or historical affinities that make the risks seem smaller, even if they
are not. Typically, trade begins close to home and then, as
experience and confidence grows, expands "like rings in the
water," as one official of the Stockholm Chamber of Commerce
put it.[2] The Swedes and Norwegians, for example, trade
primarily with each other, Denmark, and the United Kingdom
(a relationship that dates back to the Vikings). French firms
trade mostly within the European Community and with former

French colonies in Africa. And even in Germany, the export powerhouse, Ministry of Industry officials complain that many SMEs export only to European Community members.[3]

Beyond these psychological barriers lie myriad practical barriers to successful export market development. How can small companies with limited resources acquire accurate information on emerging market opportunities and develop live trade leads? How can such companies obtain reliable intelligence on competition in foreign markets? How can they learn about pricing strategies and distribution systems? How do they go about identifying potential representatives or joint venture partners? And how can they shoulder the transaction costs, once they are ready to export, without risking the stability of the firm?

Few studies of nonexporting SMEs identify the barriers these firms feel are most difficult to overcome, perhaps because it is hard to identify a sample of SMEs that have both considered and rejected exporting. However, several studies have been done on the relative importance of different export barriers to SMEs that do export.[4] While the findings vary slightly, the studies share several conclusions. The principal hurdles appear to be obtaining market intelligence, setting prices, finding representatives, completing the required export documentation and other paperwork, and negotiating satisfactory payment terms.

Governments are limited, at least technically, in how far they can go to help firms overcome these barriers and succeed at exporting by the terms of the General Agreement on Trade and Tariffs (GATT). Direct government subsidies that would reduce the buyer's price are prohibited, but a wide range of promotional activities is permitted, including support for market research and other programs that provide information on export opportunities, trade missions, and trade fair participation; permanent overseas trade promotion offices, government-sponsored R&D of exportable products, trade finance, insurance, and free trade zones; and rebates on indirect taxes (such as value-added tax) paid by the seller, but not of direct taxes on profit or property.[5]

Within the limits of this general framework, however, most European nations have been able to construct comprehensive systems of public and private export assistance services that enable SMEs to overcome external barriers to trade. The specific services available are designed to overcome barriers to obtaining market intelligence, gaining market exposure, and securing market entry.

While some programs are new and specifically target export-ready firms, others have been in place for some time and are available to any firm, export ready or not, that meets the basic qualifications. Consequently, some firms benefit more from these forms of assistance than others. But all the programs address specific barriers to export growth with equally specific forms of assistance. And the trend is toward even more specificity in the future.

## Overcoming Market Intelligence Barriers

> Small businesses seldom have any intelligence-gathering apparatus; they need access to the right information, in the right form, at the right time.
> *Dr. Gunter Kayser, Institute for Research on Medium-Sized Businesses, Bonn*

Every industrialized nation collects trade statistics, information on overseas market structures and trends (often by both country and sector), and trade leads. In some countries, entire agencies are dedicated solely to analyzing, packaging, and disseminating trade-related data. Germany's Office of Trade Information, for example, is widely recognized for the quality of its trade analyses, though German export officials complain that the organization's capabilities and products are not widely known within Germany. In other countries, the collection and processing of trade information is generally assigned to the export promotion agency as part of a portfolio of responsibilities that also includes counseling and promotion. France's Center for Foreign Commerce (CFCE), Italy's Institute for Foreign Trade (ICE), and Britain's Overseas Trade Board (BOTB) operate in this manner.

Market data reports, such as the Country Profiles and Sector Reports produced by the British Export Market Information Centre, are typically distributed by mail, for a fee. Access to trade agency databases is often possible at agency branch offices, as is the case with the U.S. and Foreign Commercial Service (US&FCS, the U.S. government's export assistance outreach program), but at present only France permits individuals direct electronic access to its database.

In addition to conducting general market and sector studies, these organizations also gather trade leads collected by sources such as commercial staff at embassies and consulates, overseas chambers of commerce, and overseas trade offices and match those leads with companies identified in their computerized directories as interested in such data.[6] This information is disseminated either by mail (generally within twenty-four hours) or electronically, as with the U.S. Department of Commerce's Trade Opportunities Program, which promises subscribers not simply prescreened direct sales leads, but also offers of representation, investment opportunities, licensing partners, joint venture partners, project bids, and foreign government tenders.[7] Regional and national chambers of commerce, private service providers, including banks, accounting firms, and trade lead services, and even international organizations, such as the European Community's European Information Centres and Business Cooperation Network ("BC-NET"), also offer market opportunity data or connect would-be exporters with potential buyers and trading partners.[8] Few of these services are free, though services provided by public bodies may be priced below market levels (see chapter 6).

The problem with many of these market intelligence services, according to users, is that the information they provide is often out of date. For example, according to the BOTB's

Quality Management System (currently the only national export service evaluation system), Britain's Export Intelligence Service (EIS), the first of the national automated trade lead systems, has the lowest satisfaction rate of any of the advice, information, or promotion services BOTB provides.[9] According to another independent EIS evaluation, "most subscribers found this service in general to be far too late for primary-information use and particularly for the early stages of project information."[10] Similar comments have been made about the trade lead and market data services of other countries as well.

There is a certain inevitability to this dissatisfaction. In a world where instantaneous global communication has become commonplace, such market data are almost certain to be out of date. Moreover, the atomization of markets into narrow niches makes acquiring useful market intelligence more difficult than ever for firms, and providing useful intelligence difficult for national export assistance organizations, whether public or private.

Consequently, while the major trading nations continue to collect and disseminate trade data as a mechanism for helping firms overcome informational barriers to exporting, some European nations have also created programs that provide individual SMEs with detailed and timely market intelligence specific to their needs, through market research consultancies partly subsidized by government or government/industry partnerships.

### PROGRAM PROFILE
*Market Research Consultancies*

It is not clear that Britain's version of the market research consultancy, the Export Market Research Scheme (EMRS), is a direct response to dissatisfaction with the BOTB's Export Intelligence Service, but it certainly is designed to address some of the weaknesses of that program. Under EMRS, firms that have fewer than 200 employees and are not divisions of other companies can get help in obtaining narrowly targeted market intelligence in one of three ways, each with government support. They can hire a private market research consultant for which the BOTB, through the Association of British Chambers of Commerce (ABCC), will pay half the cost up a maximum of nearly $40,000; the average cost is about $20,000. Firms can also do the research in house, if the ABCC feels company staff are qualified, and the government will cover half the travel-related costs of the study as long as the target market is outside the European Community, up to the same $40,000 maximum; the average cost for in-house research is about $6,000. Or firms can simply purchase published research, if it exists, with the government picking up a third of the cost, which averages less than $2,000. Roughly 600 EMRS consultancies are approved each year. To extend the program to more SMEs the government encourages trade associations to apply by covering up to 75 percent of the cost of the first research study to a maximum of about $110,000 (the government share declines for further studies).[11] According to the Quality Management System, the EMRS has the highest customer satisfaction rate of all the BOTB's advice and information services. Officials claim that, because of the specificity of the research, virtually all of the companies that have participated have successfully initiated exports to their target markets.

Denmark had a similar consultancy program in place until 1990, when it was superseded by an export network development initiative. Under the original Export Market Development Program, the government provided soft loans of 40 to 60 percent of the cost of researching a targeted market. The average loan was $140,000 over three years. To encourage collaboration and increase the reach of the investment, the program was limited to groups of three or more firms with less than $500,000 in exports to a given market. If the research resulted in successful exporting, the loan was to be repaid through a 3 to 10 percent royalty on sales over a three- to five-year period. As of 1990, some 650 such programs had been

approved, and repayment—and therefore success—was running at about 30 percent a year in 1989.[12]

Since 1989, France has also operated a subsidized market
research consultancy fund, Regional Assistance and Consultancy Fund (FRAC). Under the FRAC-Export component of
this program, SMEs may apply to either a regional government
or, in the Paris and Ile de France regions, the regional chamber
of commerce and industry, for assistance in hiring a marketing
consultant to undertake a customized study of a target export
market. If the application is approved, the government supports up to 50 percent of the cost of consulting assistance, to
a maximum of about $30,000; the average cost is about
$10,000. The Paris chamber alone funds between 100 and 150
FRAC-Export consultancies a year.

German trade officials assert that the government provides
no direct subsidies for SME export market development, leaving the task entirely to the country's powerful Association of
Chambers of Industry and Commerce (IHK), and its affiliate
bilateral Chambers of Commerce Abroad (AHK). But this
statement obscures the fact that the federal and state governments do participate indirectly in funding some of the work
of the chambers, such as export market research. In eleven of
the German states, for example, SMEs interested in obtaining
intelligence on a given market opportunity can apply to their
local IHK office for an analysis conducted by the AHK, with
25 to 30 percent of the cost of the study subsidized by the
state Ministry of Industry. In addition, companies can obtain
through their local chamber a range of market studies, including tailored analyses, from the government's Office of
Trade Information. The fees member firms pay for such studies
do not represent the full cost of producing them.[13]

In each of these cases, dissatisfaction with the utility of
generic market and trade lead data has moved many European
countries to establish programs that help SMEs obtain or
develop their own narrowly targeted market intelligence specific to their needs, with the governments absorbing some of
the cost.

## Overcoming Market Exposure Barriers

> We cannot sell the products for companies, only expose
> them to the markets.
> *Willy Stahl, Economic Development Corporation, North Rhine-
> Westphalia*

Gaining market exposure is the step between gathering intelligence on market opportunities and actually implementing a
market penetration plan. It is, in effect, the second necessary
stage of intelligence-gathering that familiarizes a firm with the
structure, operation, and players in a new market and, through
that intelligence, reduces the risk of market entry. But the
barriers to market exposure for SMEs are significant. Small
firms typically cannot afford the luxury of having the chief
executive travel extensively to explore new markets or of hiring
an export consultant to do the job on the company's behalf.

Consequently, several European governments have created
or helped sponsor opportunities for small firms to "get their
feet wet" in export markets: by directly subsidizing travel
expenses incurred while exploring new markets, by covering
some of the participation costs for trade fairs and trade missions,
by bringing buyers from foreign markets to the home country,
and by representing SMEs through overseas offices and hosting
firm members when they visit. Of these, market exploration
and trade fair participation programs offer the most interesting
initiatives.

### PROGRAM PROFILE
*Assisted Market Exposure*

France may be the most aggressive supporter of market exploration in Europe. To encourage SMEs to develop overseas markets, the state-owned French Insurance Company for Foreign
Trade (COFACE) will reimburse 50 percent (more in difficult
markets) of the costs of two individual missions by up to
three company executives for as long as two weeks.[14] More

significantly, for an annual premium equal to 1.5 percent of an SME's market exploration budget, COFACE will guarantee from 50 to 60 percent of the cost of market exploration activities, up to approximately $160,000, if subsequent export income from the target market fails to cover R&D costs.[15] Repayment is graduated over six years to keep pace with anticipated business growth. A similar program for large firms guarantees up to 75 percent with repayment over ten years. According to one COFACE official, some 6,000 firms have participated in this guarantee program, and two-thirds have been either wholly or partly successful.[16] In a related scheme, for SMEs producing innovative (generally high-tech) products with export potential, COFACE will guarantee up to 75 percent of the cost of market studies, through the National Agency for Research and Expansion, or ANVAR.[17] Finally, regional organizations associated with—and in some cases supported by—regional governments in France provide additional market research subsidies (see chapter 5).

The government is perhaps more directly involved in trade fair and related export event sponsorship in France than in any other European nation. Through the French Committee for External Economic Events (CFME), France sponsors or helps organize representation in more than 200 trade events each year, including sector- or country-specific trade fairs, French pavilions in international expositions, in-store promotions, technology expositions, and targeted missions abroad. Sometimes these government-organized events are sponsored jointly with other organizations, such as regional chambers of commerce or trade associations, sometimes in competition with them. They are unquestionably France's principal export promotion activity; nearly 4,000 enterprises were represented at CFME-sponsored events in 1989.[18] Exhibitors, however, are not directly subsidized and are expected to pay all costs of participation, in advance, including their share of booth or pavilion fees. But any risk in non-EC fairs is substantially reduced by another COFACE insurance scheme: for a premium equal to 2 percent of the approved trade fair participation

budget, COFACE will guarantee 50 to 60 percent of the cost
if sales have not exceeded costs after two to three years.[19]

In Britain the BOTB also encourages firms to gain market
exposure by participating in such events as trade fairs, international expositions, in-store promotions, trade missions, and
overseas seminars. In a recent change of policy, however, the
BOTB now leaves the organization of these activities primarily
to chambers of commerce and trade associations. But it is much
more active than the French government in directly subsidizing
the costs of participating in such events. The BOTB picks up
50 percent of the cost to firms of establishing booths at fairs
and permits them to receive assistance as often as three times
in a given market. Roughly 8,000 individuals were subsidized
to participate in nearly 350 fairs during the 1989–90 fiscal
year.[20] Additional subsidies are available for participation in
trade missions, store promotions, and trade seminars. The
BOTB even has a New Products from Britain program that
subsidizes the cost of generating publicity for specific products
in target markets.[21] Britain provides even more generous subsidies when foreign buyers participate in an "inward mission"
sponsored by representatives of British industry—chambers of
commerce, trade associations, or trade fair sponsors, for example. The BOTB will pay 50 to 75 percent of the cost of business
and in some cases first-class airfare, 50 percent of travel expenses
in Britain, interpreters' fees, and briefing and debriefing lunch
or dinner receptions. It will even provide a lodging subsidy.

Trade fairs are Germany's principal method of providing
opportunities for market exposure to SMEs. Organizing and
managing trade fairs is big business in Germany, and a private
organization, the Confederation of German Trade Fair and
Exhibition Industries (AUMA) acts as the umbrella organization for several dozen private sector fair organizers, chambers of
commerce, and trade associations. Each year, AUMA identifies,
screens, and rates more than 2,500 trade fairs and exhibitions
held around the world and oversees German participation in a
select group of them. In addition, it helps organize, and
oversees, more than a hundred fairs held each year within

Germany, involving more than 100,000 exhibitors and draw-
ing nearly 10 million participants.[22] So effective is AUMA at
these tasks that it has become the de facto trade fair expert for
the entire European Community. German export officials view
trade fairs not only as the best way for SMEs to gain low-risk
exposure to new market opportunities, but also as an important
method of displaying the excellence of German products to
the world. Depending on the cost of each fair, the German
government subsidizes roughly 30 percent of the cost of participation, channeling these funds through the fair organizers.
Any firm can qualify for assistance.[23] In addition, as part of a
Fitness for Europe campaign aimed at the coming Single
Market, the government has set aside several million deutsche
marks annually to encourage groups of SMEs to participate in
fairs within Europe.[24] Several of the German states also subsi-
dize trade fair participation; North Rhine-Westphalia, for
example, spends between 60 and 65 percent of its roughly $3
million annual export promotion budget on trade fairs and will
cover nearly 50 percent of the cost of setting up and staffing
exhibit booths.[25]

---

### TRADE FAIRS: ARE THEY WORTH IT?

The entrenched position of the trade fairs in the government support
system contributes to diverting the attention of both exporters and export promotion agencies from other potentially more profitable marketing tools.
*Carl Arthur Solberg, Norwegian School of Management*

In both Europe and the United States, trade fairs and exhibitions are typically the most heavily used tool for encouraging
SMEs to export. These activities are attractive ways to gain
market exposure for several reasons. They are a low-risk way
for firms to present their products to many potential buyers at
a small per-contact cost. Properly presented, these events offer
SMEs a level of visibility that would otherwise be difficult to
achieve. Fairs also give firms a quick read on their competi-

tion. And they give inexperienced firms a chance to interact with and learn from more seasoned participants.

It is difficult to obtain activity-by-activity breakdowns of export promotion budgets, but where such information is available, the dominance of trade fairs is hard to ignore. More than half of the budget for export promotion in Norway, for example, is devoted to trade fair support.[26] In the United Kingdom, just under half of the BOTB's nonstaff expenditures (net of receipts) goes to trade fairs.[27] On the private sector side, chambers of commerce and trade associations invest heavily in trade fair participation and assistance. When the U.S. National Association of State Development Agencies (NASDA) asked its membership in 1990 what overseas activities they emphasized, trade fairs came out on top. Moreover, NASDA discovered that several states, including Colorado, Indiana, Kansas, South Dakota, and Wyoming, had established European-style trade fair subsidy programs, often covering as much as 50 percent of a company's expenses at approved international trade shows, with caps ranging from $2,000 to $5,000.[28]

In many sectors and markets, the utility of trade fairs is taken as an article of faith. But do they work? Few countries or states know. Some officials offer anecdotal information on sales generated by trade fairs, but a blanket causal relationship is hard to prove, long-term impact is unclear, and—more important—no country has attempted to determine whether investment in trade fairs is more or less effective than other export promotion techniques. Norway examined its trade fair support system and found that, while 80 percent of the firms surveyed said they would not participate without a subsidy, the subsidy itself was minuscule, averaging only 0.2 of 1 percent of companies' annual export sales; that 60 percent of participants failed to follow up leads from fairs; that half the participants were either neutral or negative about the results of participation; and that most participants were not new-to-market SMEs but well-established exporting firms, which had been participating and being subsidized for many years.[29] Norway has since tightened eligibility for subsidized participation, requiring evidence of a marketing plan and limiting repeat attendance, among other things.

There is indirect evidence that other countries are trying to improve the payoff from trade fairs as well. In Germany—Europe's self-described "trade fair country"—the AUMA now encourages firms to do market research in advance of attendance.[30] The state of North Rhine-Westphalia requires participants to attend prefair roundtable discussions and talks by specialists in the market covered by the fair.[31] Recently, regional organizations in France (though not the national organizations) have begun to move away from trade fairs, preferring instead to emphasize direct negotiations with potential trade partners as a faster and more efficient way of gaining market exposure.

In the end, however, the question of whether trade fairs are worth the investment may be moot. As one Danish official noted recently, "We think that trade shows are weak, but they are very visible and politicians like them."

## Overcoming Market Entry Barriers

Neither the general information, trade show, nor trade mission approach addresses the needs of a company after the initial trade opportunity is presented.[32]
*Marlene Morales, XPORT, Port Authority of New York and New Jersey*

What distinguishes export promotion from export assistance—and sets many U.S. programs apart from the best European programs—is focus. Export promotion programs are aimed at overcoming motivational and informational barriers, while export assistance programs work to overcome informational and transactional barriers. Transactional barriers involve the nuts and bolts of exporting, the arrangements needed to close an export deal—from establishing representation or arranging joint ventures to addressing credit and finance, insurance, shipping, standards, and customs requirements.

This is a crucial distinction, because in the absence of effective transactional assistance, SMEs lured into exporting by motivational programs and encouraged to get their feet wet through market exposure programs end up becoming episodic, ineffective exporters. According to one U.S. export policy expert, for many SMEs the toughest hurdle is not the difficulty or cost of acquiring information on export market opportunities, but the transactional costs involved in negotiating and executing a shipment.[33] Not surprisingly, researchers have found that exporters are more interested in services that address transactional barriers than in any other form of assistance.[34]

The major European exporting nations offer the full range of export transaction services, in sharp contrast to the fragmented and incomplete transactional infrastructure in the United States. But it is also true that perhaps in no other area of export policy are there such sharp differences among European nations. The methods of providing these transactional services to exporters in general and SME exporters in particular vary according to the philosophy of each country's government.

At one extreme is France, whose government is involved directly (typically through government chartered quasi-independent corporations) in almost every aspect of servicing export transactions. At the other extreme is Germany, whose government has little direct involvement with the nuts and bolts of such services, leaving them instead to a well-integrated system dominated by the domestic and overseas chambers of commerce, banks, shipping companies, and trading houses. The government plays only a minor role as a guarantor in certain kinds of financial transactions.

Most other European nations fall somewhere between these two extremes. In Sweden, for example, the Swedish Trade Council (jointly run and funded by government and industry) provides a wide range of technical services to its members at a discount and to others at full cost. The council offers help with locating overseas representatives, establishing subsidiaries, acquiring companies, securing licenses, negotiating joint ventures, and recruiting personnel. It can also assist companies with the complexities of export standards, liability and other trade laws, customs and documentation, shipping, and payment terms. Export finance and insurance, however, are left to private institutions.

In addition to those services discussed elsewhere, Britain uses a mix of public and private entities to help SMEs overcome market entry barriers. The Foreign Service identifies and screens potential overseas representatives for new exporters, while a Simpler Trade Procedures (SITPRO) Board helps firms sort out export documentation and an Export Credits Guarantee Department (ECGD) provides insurance coverage against the full range of financial risks. Private chambers of commerce, which serve as the official access points for some public services, also connect exporters to banks, shipping companies, and private export consultants and act as the designated authority for the issuance of certificates of origin and similar documents.

### PROGRAM PROFILE
*France's Agency for the International Promotion of SMEs*

Perhaps the most interesting example in Europe of the trend toward direct market entry assistance is France's Agency for the International Promotion of SMEs (API-PME). Created in 1978 as a spin-off from the General Federation of SMEs (a not-for-profit lobbying association), API-PME exists solely to help SMEs test and enter new export markets. API-PME has seventeen offices in fifteen countries around the world, often shared with French Trade Commission offices, and a total staff of about fifty people, half of them in Paris. These overseas branches identify market sectors in which export opportunities exist for French firms, then work through the federation's membership to find firms interested in entering those markets. API-PME takes this active rather than reactive approach to market development explicitly to overcome the historical resistance of French SMEs to venturing outside the domestic market, according to API-PME's former New York office director Fabrice Taupin, but SMEs interested in exporting may also approach API-PME independently.

Following an initial audit of a firm to determine its export readiness, API-PME will test market the firm's product(s) in a particular market, exploring customer reactions, assessing competition, reviewing design compatibility, and advising on packaging and pricing, among other issues. Depending on the strategy a company interested in entering the market prefers, API-PME will identify potential importers and distribution partners, gather intelligence on potential joint venture partners or acquisitions, or help the company sort out the geographic, legal, and regulatory issues associated with establishing a subsidiary operation in the market.

API-PME provides direct market entry assistance to roughly eighty companies each year. The assistance typically lasts two to three years, after which the companies are able to stand alone. Fees for these services range from roughly $1,500 for a market test to as much as $10,000 for partner searches. On the other hand, API-PME will do all the paperwork necessary for its clients to receive national government export assistance, such as FRAC grants and COFACE insurance coverage, at no charge. API-PME's fees are more attractive than those of private consultants because it is a not-for-profit organization. Its operating costs are low because it shares the French Trade Commission offices overseas, and its personnel and indirect costs are covered by the fees paid by the General Federation of SMEs' 1.5 million members.

But according to the organization's current New York representative, Olivier Touzé, API-PME's principal competitive advantage is that it is able to *travailler sur le terrain*, or work on the ground. It knows its markets well and can significantly reduce the transactional risks SMEs face when they decide to enter a new export market.

## EXPORT FINANCE: ANOTHER OF EUROPE'S COMPETITIVE ADVANTAGES

It is extremely difficult—if not impossible—for a small business in this country to get any kind of export financing.[35]
*Rep. Norman Sisisky, chairman, House Subcommittee on Exports, Tax Policy, and Special Problems*

No deal is too small for us.[36]
*Daniel J. Harwood, Copenhagen HandelsBanken*

It's possible to spend weeks in Europe exploring small business export problems and never once hear a complaint about export finance. On the other hand, it's just as possible to go anywhere in the United States to discuss exporting and hear nothing but complaints about the lack of export finance. The money shortage is neither the only nor the most important barrier to increased U.S. exporting, but it so dominates the debate that it obscures all others. One expert notes wryly, "By commenting that export financing has gone from bad to worse, we run the risk of perpetuating the myth of the existence of an infrastructure in the US market for export financing. Such an infrastructure does not exist."[37]

Exporters need financing to cover the production costs even before an order is shipped, to pay for export receivables (which typically have much longer payment terms than domestic accounts), and to serve as insurance against economic and political risks. While European SME exporters can turn either to government-owned or -backed financial institutions or to their own banks, U.S. firms, for the most part, can turn to neither. Government export finance agencies—principally the Export-Import Bank (Eximbank) and the Small Business Administration—have been criticized repeatedly as underfunded, bureaucratic, and oriented principally toward medium-sized and large transactions. Recent well-intentioned efforts by these organizations to improve their performance have been hampered by a lack of resources. Thus, while national export finance agencies elsewhere in the developed world cover an average of 15 percent of all export transactions, the Eximbank covers less than 2 percent of U.S. transactions.[38] To make matters worse, few banks are willing to handle Eximbank guarantees. Most of Europe's export financing is handled by private or state-owned banks. State-owned banks provide financing for small export transactions as a matter of policy, despite the small payoff. Private banks view the high cost of small transactions as a loss leader. According to Deutsche Bank official Wolfgang Bongertz, "It's no secret that it is more costly to service a number of small deals than a single large one, but we see it as an investment in firms with the potential to become good customers in the future."[39] Additionally, most European banks are part of a global network. "We are linked to more than 10,000 cooperating banks," says Copenhagen HandelsBanken's Daniel J. Harwood, "but not one in the U.S."[40]

U.S. banks have never developed the international trade finance orientation and expertise of their European counterparts. Small banks do not have the capacity to handle international deals, and large banks that do have the capacity refuse to handle small transactions. In some regions, the minimum transaction large banks will consider is $1 million, far larger than all but a tiny percentage of export deals.[41] And after sustaining heavy losses in the developing world during the 1980s, many large banks have closed down their international operations altogether.

Increasingly in the United States, export finance authorities are being created at the state level in an effort to fill the gap. By 1990, enabling legislation had been passed in twenty-one states. But operational programs that provide loans, guarantees, insurance, or some combination existed in only fifteen of these states, and only five states (California, Illinois, Maryland, Minnesota, and New York) had authorizations large enough to make a difference for would-be exporters.[42] In addition, in 1992 nineteen states and two cities were participating in Eximbank's City/State Program, designed to make the bank's guarantees more accessible to SMEs. Increasing accessibility will do little, however, to overcome Eximbank's limited resources or the lack of interest commercial banks have shown in Eximbank guarantees.

The inescapable conclusion is that, even if all public financing programs authorized at the state and federal level in the United States were working effectively, they would not approach the level of assistance available to SMEs in many European countries. Even taking into consideration countries where private banks provide most of the export finance, the United States has no comparable range of services at any price. Given these constraints, companies are left with only one option: to finance export sales from their own cash reserves—a risky strategy given the usual terms for foreign receivables. As *INC.* magazine concluded in a recent review of the export financing problem, "Our infrequent exporters may be exporting so little because that's all they can afford to finance internally. And they have no other funding options."[43]

---

## Lesson 6: *Most national export assistance programs are too general to be effective; the most effective programs are deep, specific, and customized to individual firms.*

SMEs lack the capacity to assimilate and use general information on export opportunities.
*Svante Blomqvist, Swedish Trade Council*

Eventually, companies that want to export need tailor-made help, but they cannot get it from national agencies.
*Enrico Ricotta, Strategie & Accordi S.r.l., Rome*

Common sense suggests that assistance services should be tailored to the needs of the firms that require help, but common sense has not been common practice. In the past, export assistance programs on both sides of the Atlantic have tended not only to be aimed broadly at all SMEs, as if these firms were monolithic, but also to offer the same basic services, as if their needs were essentially generic. A recent study by the European Commission concluded, "Assistance and inducements from the support agencies should not be aimed at the macro level but . . . specifically tailored to the stage each firm has reached in the export process. An analogy would be that help be custom built rather than mass produced." The same study found that the average support agency is not sufficiently market oriented.[44]

A recent study of the export promotion programs of ten American states arrived at a similar conclusion, noting, "Overall, it appears that state agencies charged with the task of promoting exports from their state pay very little attention to tailoring export promotion programs to varying exporter needs. The states currently use a universal approach to export promotion instead of a perhaps more effective segmented approach."[45] The export assistance needs of SMEs are neither generic nor universal, but vary widely according to the stage of export-readiness a firm has attained. Not surprisingly, therefore, another recent study concluded, "There often exists a poor match between the assistance needs of companies and the programs provided."[46]

Many European nations still offer a wide range of largely untargeted export assistance programs for SMEs. France and Britain, where the government's role is strongest, have the most comprehensive programs. But officials in these countries express frustration with the limitations of these generic programs. French regional officials and their SME customers describe the complex French export assistance system as bureaucratic, unwieldy, and time-consuming. In Britain, despite the relatively high customer satisfaction ratings provided by the BOTB's Quality Management System, some officials confess, "The help we can offer is really help at the margins."[47] In the Netherlands, exporting SMEs surveyed in 1983 characterized national export assistance agencies as bureaucratic, slow, detached, and ill informed about SME needs.[48]

Partly in response to these complaints, and partly because

tight national budgets have forced closer scrutiny of programs long taken for granted, comprehensive national export assistance initiatives are beginning to change. Britain, for example, has shifted some services from government agencies to the chambers of commerce and now aims to offer "only those services government can best provide."[49] In 1989 France created a National Export Charter that brought together the many public, private, national, and regional export assistance bodies for a coordinated campaign to penetrate British, German, and Spanish export markets.

But these changes are occurring slowly. In the meantime, a new generation of customer-driven export assistance programs has emerged in Europe, often organized at the regional level and delivered by private or quasi-private organizations, with financial assistance from regional governments. While national programs tend to be broad, these new initiatives are narrow, aimed at overcoming specific barriers in specific markets for specific industrial sectors. While national programs tend to be universal, these new programs are customized for individual firms. While the help offered in national programs tends to be shallow, the new programs are thorough, taking participating firms all the way from export strategy development to signing contracts with overseas partners.

Just as the most competitive industries have shifted from the Tayloristic model of mass production to a narrower, flexible niche-market production model, SME export assistance programs have moved from mass-produced assistance to targeted, flexible, customized "niche" programs. These programs seldom concern themselves with motivating SMEs to begin exporting, focusing instead on helping export-ready firms overcome informational and transactional barriers in specific markets. Such an approach sacrifices scope (reaching large numbers of firms) to achieve impact (ensuring that clients succeed in penetrating their target markets).

Examples of the trend toward customized export assistance programs can be found in most European countries, and in the United States, at XPORT, the trading company of the Port

Authority of New York and New Jersey. SVEX and RESFOR, the service centers of the Emilia-Romagna region of Italy, provide deep, tailored assistance. Germany's chambers of commerce and commercial banks have long worked together to do the same, as has the Swedish Trade Council. One project in France, however, perhaps best captures the mix of public, private, regional, and national characteristics of these customized export initiatives.

### PROGRAM PROFILE
*Brittany's MIRCEB*

In 1982, following the election of France's first socialist government, a massive transfer of power and resources from the central government gave regional governments significant new responsibilities for economic development. In Brittany, a group of private businesses established the Regional Mission for the Coordination of International Trade with Brittany (MIRCEB) to fill a void in public services. MIRCEB provides tailored assistance to help the region's small firms become exporters and, in the process, strengthen the regional economy. According to MIRCEB's Director Michel Chabrat, "We concluded we could solve our unemployment problem only by creating growing, widely based international market opportunities and helping firms develop the skill and flexibility to move into them."[50]

On a fee-for-service basis, MIRCEB offers Breton firms foreign market studies, assistance in preparing for trade fairs and exhibitions, counseling on preparing export strategies, searches for overseas representatives, contacts with and evaluation of joint venture partners, subsidiary plant location, foreign company acquisition, and technology transfers, among other services. It also covers, through the regional government, up to 30 percent of the cost of any export-related activity to a maximum of roughly $8,000 per year for up to three years. Some 60 to 70 percent of MIRCEB's current budget comes from the Breton government, much of it in the form of the 30 percent market development subsidy; the rest comes from client fees and corporate contributions.

MIRCEB has no fixed menu of services. Instead, it draws up a customized contract with an individual firm to penetrate an individual market. The package of services is tailored to the company's needs and designed to reduce both the entry risk and the time needed to get established. Norman Arends, a transplanted Texan who oversees MIRCEB's three U.S. offices, is contemptuous of traditional export promotion techniques: "Trade fairs and missions are nothing more than paid vacations, and conferences and seminars are a waste of time; you need the right people located in the target market to broker deals for the client."[51]

With a headquarters staff of ten and twelve other representatives posted in the United States, Asia, and Europe, MIRCEB has been able to change the growth rates of its clients dramatically through export development. Between 1984 and 1988, for example, MIRCEB increased its clients' sales 400 percent, while sales of all Breton companies increased only 50 percent. According to Chabrat, MIRCEB's experience suggests five keys to helping small firms penetrate export markets:

—Find the right fit—MIRCEB locates the right market and the right trading partner for the client firm.

—Be customer oriented—MIRCEB works the same hours, talks the same language, and has the same rhythm as its clients. The customer determines the program, not the other way around.

—Interact with the client—MIRCEB maintains day-to-day contact with its clients and changes its strategy as their needs change.

—Customize the services offered—MIRCEB has no generic forms of assistance; the services provided are those demanded by the deal as it develops.

—Be flexible—both MIRCEB's services and the markets in which its branches are located can be, and have been, changed as the needs of clients require.

MIRCEB's flexibility is illustrated by a recent change in

its strategy. When it became clear that simply helping Breton firms export through distributorships provided little feedback on product sales and additional market opportunities, MIRCEB shifted its emphasis to two-way trade opportunities, joint ventures, technology-sharing, and product lines developed jointly by Breton and overseas firms.

The point, according to Chabrat, is that focusing on both sides of the trade equation "helps MIRCEB firms and their foreign partners develop a symbiotic relationship—a network of shared experiences, contacts, and product ideas" that continuously generates new business possibilities.[52] Others have learned the same lesson.

### Lesson 7: *The real issue isn't exporting, but increasing trade flow within the global economy.*

International trade is not a one-way street.
*Helga Massow, Managing Director, Foreign Trade
Promotion Institute, North Rhine-Westphalia*

German trade officials are quick to point out that they are as interested in increasing imports as they are in increasing exports. In part, this attitude stems from the need to balance the country's chronic trade surpluses in manufactured goods. But it is also an indirect expression of how vulnerable even the Germans feel they are to accelerating competition in the European and global economies. While this vulnerability has produced a degree of protectionism in the past, the scenario is changing.[53] With more "neighbors" arrayed along its borders than any other European nation—neighbors that constitute potential competition as well as markets—Germany understands perhaps more clearly than any other industrialized nation that competitiveness depends on the free flow of products, technology, and ideas among countries—in short, of trade, not just exports. Thus, Germany's 43 Chambers of Commerce Abroad (AHK) are organized as bilateral trade development bodies rather than as export promoters. Of the AHK's 40,000 member firms around the world, three-fifths are not German. German firms are not just increasing their exports, but are trying to build trade relationships.

The intensification of global economic competition, and the fragmentation of markets into narrow niches that form and reform as consumer demands shift and technology changes, places significant burdens on would-be SME exporters. Export assistance officials in several European countries have concluded that inflexibility—in either product design or export distribution mechanisms—often dooms export initiatives to marginality or failure.

The easiest route to exporting, and the one most commonly taken by smaller firms, is simply to unload an existing product line through a distributor, a trading house, or some other passive form of representation. More than a third of the inquiries on BC-Net for the month of June 1990 were requests for or offers to provide distribution and sales agent services.[54] Moreover, the practice of customizing products for individual markets is still relatively limited, even in Europe. A recent European Commission study, for example, found that even among successful frequent exporters, only half of the firms surveyed tailored products to market specifications.[55]

This "one-way street" approach to trade is flawed in several respects. First, it often incorrectly assumes that consumers in foreign markets will accept products in unmodified form. Second, it utilizes trade channels (distributors, agents, and trading houses) that may provide little, if any, feedback on sales, buyer responses, or market trends. Third, it misses opportunities to reduce the cost of product development and market penetration by using in-the-market partners. Fourth, it forfeits opportunities for the exchange of innovation. The result is that companies seldom know why a product has succeeded or failed in a given market and have no way to obtain intelligence on changes in the marketplace, including emerging competitors, that could affect future sales. In short, what looks initially like a low-risk strategy often becomes a high-risk one.

While national agencies and chambers of commerce con-

tinue to pursue export promotion strategies such as trade fairs
and missions that may perpetuate these weaknesses, some state
and regional agencies, often assisted by private or quasi-private
organizations, have begun to develop more sophisticated trade
relationships among smaller firms. MIRCEB is one example of
a trade development partnership between public and private
entities—one that grew out of dissatisfaction with the limitations of conventional export promotion.

There are other examples, including northern Italy's flexible manufacturing networks and associated service centers
such as SVEX, and North Rhine-Westphalia's Foreign Trade
Institute, which pools private and public resources to cultivate
international trade-related partnerships. In these and other
European programs, a pattern emerges that suggests a transi-
tion from narrow export promotion programs to reciprocal
trade relationships that function as learning systems for their
participants. Not surprisingly, this shift in objective has neces-
sitated a shift in techniques, placing even greater emphasis on
the need for transactional assistance. Another French initiative,
a joint effort of the Essonne regional government and a private
management consulting firm, illustrates this trend.

## PROGRAM PROFILE
### Essonne's "Objective Europe" Project

The Essonne department of France, south of Paris, is home to
some 40 percent of France's high-tech businesses and R&D
centers. In 1990, faced with the impending integration of the
Single European Market, Essonne's economic development
board concluded that the firms forming the backbone of the
region's economy needed a trade presence elsewhere in Europe
in order to remain competitive. The board also concluded that
the firms themselves were unlikely to find time to explore
markets, screen potential joint venture partners, and negotiate
contracts. Instead, the board hired DML & Associates, a Paris-
based international management consulting firm with expertise
in regional economic development, to act as a broker for the

region's firms and potential joint venture partners. Called "Objective Europe," the joint public and private team developed a four-stage process designed to lead quickly to concrete trade, production, and technology-sharing agreements. The first target market was Great Britain.

In stage one, DML invited 1,000 Essonne SMEs to a meeting to explore internationalization opportunities. Some 300 firms attended. Through interviews and a detailed questionnaire, DML did a preliminary management audit to determine which SMEs were both willing and financially able to make a serious commitment. Forty firms met the criteria and, with DML's assistance, developed individualized strategic plans for approaching the U.K. market. Few of the firms were just starting up, but many were young, with annual turnovers ranging from $5 million to $20 million. In stage two, using profiles provided by the French firms, DML's London office identified some fifteen potential British joint venture partners for each firm, then arranged for the managing directors of the French firms to meet with and assess their potential partners at a central U.K. location. At stage three, British firms interested in pursuing ventures with their French counterparts were invited to France to begin direct negotiations, with DML acting as broker. Finally, at stage four, DML began executing binding contracts between firms from the two countries. Less than ten months after the initial meeting, eight of the original forty firms had signed contracts. Seven more were actively negotiating and expected to sign contracts.

The total cost of the project, less than $500,000, was split between the Essone government and the French Ministry of Industry. A "success fee" was charged to each of the firms that reached the contract stage and the proceeds were returned to the regional government. So pleased was the Essonne government that a similar process is already underway to develop partnerships with German firms. The only major change in the methodology will involve having participating firms put some of their own money on the table at the outset.[56]

## Chapter 5

# Who Should Deliver the Export Assistance and Where

*A walk down Düsseldorf's Immermannstrasse is a sort of global stroll. Along the broad avenue, tree lined and divided by impeccably maintained flower gardens, the glittering shops of the world's best-known fashion designers stand shoulder to shoulder with branches of the world's biggest banks and a global menu of restaurants. The pedestrian traffic is international as well. The faces you see and voices you hear are almost as likely to be Japanese as German; there are more Japanese expatriates in Düsseldorf than anywhere else in Europe—nearly 10,000 in 1990.*

*The presence of the Japanese is one of many clues to the renaissance of the German state of North Rhine-Westphalia. In the 1960s, this was the heart of Germany's coal and steel industries. Straddling the Rhine, it produced the raw materials for Germany's long climb back to industrial prominence after World War II. Then, felled by the same global structural changes that brought America's Rust Belt to its knees, the region's economy collapsed. The legacy was not promising: gray and blighted, North Rhine-Westphalia was Germany's most polluted industrial region. Yet today the state is booming. A development strategy combining basic infrastructure and amenity investments with a campaign to internationalize the state economy has made North Rhine-Westphalia the most important economic center in Germany, generating 30 percent of the nation's GNP.*

*Key elements in the state's development strategy were aggressive exporting of technology and products and importing of foreign investment. Today, a third of Germany's exports come from the state; only nine of the world's industrial countries export more than North Rhine-Westphalia.[1] In addition, it has used its strategic location and modern transportation and communications infrastructure to market itself as an ideal base for multinational companies that want a foothold in the Single European Market, attracting more than a quarter of all foreign investment in Germany, including $400 million from Japan in 1991 alone.[2]*

*Local officials credit the state's success at internationalization to the
private and quasi-private institutions that have executed much of the
development strategy. While overall policy is established by the state's
Ministry of Economics and Technology, usually in consultation with
industry and labor, execution is the responsibility of two quasi-independent
organizations: the Economic Development Corporation of North Rhine-
Westphalia and the Foreign Trade Promotion Institute, both of which
are closely connected to the state's sixteen private chambers of commerce,
six craft chambers, and many trade associations. "By listening to our
clients and speaking their language," says the Institute's Helga Massow,
"we have gone from a gray industrial region to a green industrial
region." She smiles at the double entendre.*

## Lesson 8: *Export assistance works best when it is delivered by private or quasi-private providers, with government playing an enabling role.*

Trade should not be done by diplomats or bureaucrats.
*Dr. Armin Grünewald, Association of German Chambers of
Industry and Commerce*

The export assistance philosophies of countries, states, or
regions can be characterized by the amount of public and
private sector involvement and the degree to which they are
loosely coordinated or strategically integrated.[3] The countries
discussed in this document differ significantly on each of these
characteristics.

Officially, Germany's export assistance programs are the
territory of the private sector, particularly the chambers of
industry and commerce, their overseas bilateral affiliates, the
trade associations, and the banking system. Yet state governments can and do play a role that varies from state to state, and
the federal government supports export market development to
some extent—directly in the case of the Office of Foreign Trade
Information and indirectly in the case of its contributions to
the budgets of the bilateral chambers. In addition, although
there is no identifiable public or private national export strategy

per se to coordinate the delivery of Germany's export assistance programs, it is clear that the informally structured system functions in an exceptionally integrated fashion. There is very little chance that the right hand will not know what the left is doing in the German system.

At the other extreme, France's export promotion programs are extremely centralized and dominated by the government. The Directorate of Foreign Economic Relations (DREE) controls export policy development and oversees programs managed by a bewildering array of semi-autonomous but publicly controlled agencies such as the CFCE, CFME, and COFACE, and ANVAR. The chambers of commerce—membership in which is mandatory for all firms, as it is in Germany—play a largely advisory role at the central government level. But while the national program appears highly strategic and centrally controlled, its actual operation is much less formalized. Under the regional governments, the chambers are active in serving the export assistance needs of their members. Private sector intermediary organizations, often under contract to regional governments and working closely with local chambers, play an increasing role in helping small- and medium-sized firms (SMEs) penetrate overseas markets and execute trade deals. These regional and private sector organizations are frequently scornful of the utility of the big national programs.

Italy has what can only be described as a loosely coordinated system in which a wide variety of organizations—public, private, national, and local—compete to serve the interests of export-minded SMEs. Sweden has a strongly integrated system that is roughly 50 percent public and 50 percent private and in which the roles of the various players are clearly delineated. Britain's Department of Trade and Industry has developed perhaps the most clearly presented and coherently marketed package of export assistance programs. Britain is trying to shift the administration of these once highly centralized programs to regional offices and, in some cases, to private sector service providers such as the Association of British Chambers of Commerce. But the government's resources are limited and the chambers of commerce, which are purely voluntary, are weak compared with their German and French counterparts.

Despite these differences, two themes predominate in every one of these countries. The first is that the most effective export assistance programs are those delivered by private or quasi-private organizations. This theme is so consistent that in countries such as France, where such organizations are not created explicitly for the purpose, they emerge on their own to serve SMEs.

Private sector bodies are the best deliverers of export assistance for several reasons:

—They understand the needs, the motivations, the fears, and the limits of smaller firms.

—They are in close contact with their clients and therefore are quick to sense changes in an SME's needs.

—They serve as mechanisms for relaying feedback from clients to public policymakers.

—They tend to be less subject to bureaucratic procedures that slow down decisions, tie up deals, and preclude long-term commitments.

—Rightly or wrongly, they are perceived by SMEs as having a credibility public agencies never seem to attain. In part, this is due to differences in objectives; public export agencies are motivated by matters of policy, while private organizations are oriented toward firms and their needs—and the firms know it.

—Private export assistance organizations operate in a businesslike manner that includes expecting clients to pay for services rendered (see chapter 6), and clients tend to take their own participation more seriously.

In many of the European export assistance programs profiled in the foregoing pages—Italy's SVEX, France's MIR-CEB and Essone-DML project, North Rhine-Westphalia's trade promotion programs, Britain's BOTB-Association of British Chambers of Commerce initiatives, Sweden's Trade Council—private, quasi-private, or joint public and private organizations provide the export assistance to SMEs. In Denmark the shift to private delivery has been dramatic. In 1990 the Danish Minister of Industry eliminated the government's comprehensive export market development program in favor of a new national program that fostered the creation of local and regional producer networks modeled roughly on the Emilia-Romagna model. These networks are composed of groups of private firms, brokered by private consultants, and overseen by the Danish Technology Institute (DTI); itself funded principally by private industry. The government provides modest start-up funding matched by the private sector and sets the terms for qualifying for support, but expects the networks to become self-supporting within three years. The objective, according to DTI's Niels Christian Nielsen, is to "help small companies compete together with the best of the large . . . and the number one criterion for support is that they export."[4]

The second and parallel theme that runs through countries with the most effective export assistance programs is that public sector involvement is central to assuring that the needs of SMEs are met, even when services are delivered by private organizations.

There are two reasons for government involvement in SME export assistance. The first might best be called "upward size creep." All private and public sector export assistance programs aim to meet the needs of SMEs. But over time, and in some cases right from the start, such programs invariably cater to large firms. The German chambers of commerce, for example, are criticized sharply by the German Federation of Independent Businesses (BDS) for focusing only on medium- and large-sized firms and ignoring the needs of the very small firms the BDS represents, which average between five and ten employees.[5] SME organizations in Italy, France, and Great Britain make similar complaints. In these cases, the government's role is to act as an advocate for SMEs, ensuring that their interests are represented and their needs served by the private organizations to which operational responsibility has been delegated.

The second reason for government involvement is more fundamental: market failure. The rationale for the assistance the U.K. government provides to SMEs, for example, is based upon research that reveals imperfections in both the market for export information (market awareness, market development skills, and market entry techniques) and the market for export finance.[6] So while the government is spinning functions off to the private sector—partly for policy reasons, but also because of tight national budgets—it continues to provide "those services that government can best provide to assure a level playing field" for SMEs.[7]

In practical terms, the most significant market failures may well be those associated with export transactions. Private export service providers such as banks, insurance companies, accounting firms, trading companies, and export market consultants are generally unwilling to shoulder the high costs of developing markets for SMEs without government prodding and subsidies. Even if they did, few SMEs would be able to afford the services of private providers. Consequently, governments step in to fill the gap, either directly or by providing incentives to encourage the private sector to respond. As an official of France's publicly owned export insurance agency, COFACE, explains: "It is not profitable to insure SME exports; the costs are high and the premiums they pay are low. But it is our duty because private insurers will not do it."[8]

Brittany's MIRCEB is a good example of the prevalence of these two themes. As Philippe Houchois, former manager of MIRCEB's Seattle office, testified recently before the Oregon legislature:

> MIRCEB is the result of a joint venture at two levels. The first level is a joint [venture] between the regional government that provides some funding and . . . private companies that have expressed a need for an export or trade promotion agency. At the second level, MIRCEB is a joint venture between the private companies that implicitly agree on the principle of resource-sharing.

# #

None of these companies could afford to have offices all over the world, and so they accept [sharing] the costs of these offices even if they don't need them immediately.[9]

## THE UNFULFILLED POTENTIAL OF CHAMBERS OF COMMERCE

U.S. Chamber [of commerce] trade delegations are nothing but tax-deductible excursions for CEOs and their wives. We schedule meetings at their request and many don't even bother to show up. Now we refuse to do it anymore.

*Tell Hermanson, Vice President for International Affairs, Stockholm Chamber of Commerce*

All chambers of commerce are not created equal. In several European countries, Germany, France, and Italy among them, chambers of commerce have public law status—that is, they are chartered by the government but remain independent of it. More to the point, membership in a local chamber is mandatory for all firms, generating extraordinary financial resources for programs. The German system, imposed by the French during Napoleon's occupation of the Rhineland, is the most comprehensive in Europe. Along with trade associations, eighty-three local chambers (including fourteen in eastern Germany) are the voice of business in the nation's economic affairs. They provide services ranging from the management of the nation's much-envied apprenticeship system to the promotion and development of exports. German chambers of commerce affiliates (AHK) in forty-three countries abroad provide export advice, trade leads, joint venture partner and sales representative searches, and information on customs, laws, taxation, and wage structures. Because they serve the function that in other countries is performed by the foreign service, the German government funds roughly a third of their budgets. The French and Italian systems are less comprehensive, lacking counterparts to the German overseas affiliates, for example, and the delineation of responsibility for trade development between the chambers of commerce and the government is less clear. In Italy, the chambers in the major industrial regions fund their own foreign trade assistance centers jointly with the regional government, major banks, and the local chambers.

Elsewhere, including in Britain and Sweden, membership is voluntary, as it is in the United States. But while unable to provide the same export assistance available from public law chambers of commerce (there are as many members in Stuttgart's chamber, for instance, as in the entire British system[10]), the voluntary chambers in these countries are far more active in export promotion and the provision of export market development assistance to their members than those in the United States. A firm in any of these countries can look to its local chamber for export training seminars, trade fair and trade mission assistance, trade lead data, market studies, and help with the formalities of export transactions, such as payment, shipping, and customs. The depth and quality of this assistance vary from country to country and from region to region within countries, but it dwarfs anything provided in the United States. One European chamber official comments: "U.S. chambers of commerce are neither prepared for nor interested in trade issues; our trade relationships are better with Eastern Europe than they are with the U.S. chambers."[11]

While it is easy to fault the U.S. chamber of commerce system for focusing too narrowly on lobbying and self-promotion, the public law status chambers appear to be operating below their potential as well. There is a complacency and bureaucratic stolidity about them that may well be the result of having it too easy. One French chamber official confesses that, if membership were not mandatory, "only perhaps 5 percent of all firms would participate in chamber activities."[12] Hans-Wilhelm Dunner of the Federation of Independent Businesses in Germany cites research indicating that 95 percent of new startups that receive only chamber of commerce advice fail, while only 5 percent of firms receiving "appropriate advice through consultancy arrangements" fail.[13] Elsewhere, as they do national government programs, clients criticize chambers for being dominated by large-firm issues and describe the system's export assistance programs as "too general," "superficial," or "outdated." More tellingly, the most innovative client-centered private export assistance initiatives emerging in Europe seldom arise from the chamber of commerce system.

---

## Lesson 9:  *Export assistance works best when it is regionally and sectorally targeted.*

Our national export assistance programs work best locally—where the small firm's counselor and the export advisor are the same person.
*Alison Lys, Small Firms Branch, U.K. Department of Employment*

Many of Italy's export consortia are moving from a regional focus to a focus on sectors within regions.
*Dr. Sergio Alessandrini, Bocconi University, Milan*

Call it the niche-marketing of export assistance. Just as the locus of export service delivery is shifting from government to private sector, so too the focus of that assistance is shifting from the national to the local or regional level and to specific industrial sectors within regions. The reason is simple: in country after country, export promotion officials, with declining resources and accelerating demands to make SMEs globally competitive, have had to shift their attention and their resources to those investments that will provide the biggest payoff. And their experience indicates that the more narrowly focused the assistance is, geographically and sectorally, the more tangible the results will be.

As one student of European business assistance schemes has noted, "Defining business assistance programs according to industrial sector follows the logic of the market instead of the logic of the bureaucrat."[14] The driving force in sectoral targeting is the client, not the program. Roughly the same thing can be said about regional targeting.

The logic of organizing export assistance in this manner is compelling. At the most basic level, it reflects the fact that business owners think of themselves as members of a specific industry in a specific locality or region. They have no reason to think in national terms, and nothing compels them to do so to obtain export assistance. In addition, operating at the sub-national and sector level improves the service offered by making it self-correcting; customer feedback is direct and assistance providers build expertise in both the industry and region. Moreover, natural constituencies develop that improve the political viability of the program.

Thus, the extraordinarily successful manufacturing networks of northern Italy are organized primarily within individual sectors and regions.[15] Similarly, German export assistance programs are delivered through local chambers of commerce and specific industry associations. Export programs in Britain and France, while still formulated by the government, are increasingly delivered at the regional and local levels. The overhaul of Denmark's export assistance programs embodies this principle with sweeping comprehensiveness: they now focus exclusively on the development of export-minded local business networks. And in Sweden, the Trade Council's export assistance services, as well as many other business services, reach their customers through a network of Regional Development Funds (RDFs).

## PROGRAM PROFILE
### Sectoral Targeting: Italy's RESFOR

The crux of the international trade problem for very small manufacturing firms is that they are unknown and can't afford to make themselves known. The heart of RESFOR, the Subcontractor Network for Emilia-Romagna, is a detailed and continuously updated database on the production capabilities of its member firms, which in 1989 numbered more than 600. RESFOR is able to provide any interested major manufacturer anywhere in the world with complete technical profiles on RESFOR members (80 percent of whom have fewer than twenty employees), including location and plant size, number and skills of employees, production capacity, subcontract and nonsubcontract products, range and specifications of production machinery, quality control procedures and facilities, production standards and tolerances, flexibility and specialization capacity, R&D history, patents held, business investment trend, turnover and mix, and management structure. Companies pay a membership fee of less than $250 to join RESFOR's system. Firms making inquiries receive a short printout on companies that meet their specifications, then pay for more detailed company data. RESFOR's first-year (1988) operating budget of roughly $370,000 was funded entirely by ERVET, the region's quasi-public economic development corporation, but the center is expected to be self-supporting by 1995.

The genius of RESFOR is that it also provides its members with detailed profiles on the large contractors seeking subcontractors, outlining corporate structure and history, production throughput, subcontracting practices, payment terms, and so forth. Both parties learn immediately, for a low fee, what they are getting into.

According to RESFOR Director Luciano Galletti, most of Emilia-Romagna's metalworking, rubber, plastics, and electronics subcontractors (RESFOR's target firms) are already prepared to export. By screening both buyer and seller in international subcontracting transactions, RESFOR takes much of the risk out of exporting for its members and ensures that they don't waste time on unqualified prospects. In addition, RESFOR represents member firms at international trade fairs and keeps them abreast of emerging sectoral market trends. This permits member firms to focus on production while RESFOR handles market intelligence-gathering on their behalf—in effect, bringing the market to them.

## PROGRAM PROFILE
*Geographical Targeting: Sweden's Regional Development Funds*

Firms with fewer than 200 employees constitute 99.7 percent of all businesses in Sweden and produce 25 percent of its exports, either directly or indirectly through subcontracting. To help these widely scattered SMEs gain access to the kind of public programs and private sector expertise capable of helping them reach the levels of technical quality, operational efficiency, and export-consciousness necessary to be global competitors, Sweden has established Regional Development Funds (RDFs) in each of its twenty-four counties. Originally established to furnish SMEs with high-risk capital that private banks were unwilling to provide, RDFs have since evolved to focus primarily on market-oriented development programs and on helping small businesses establish direct export operations. [16]

The RDFs embody both of the lessons presented in this chapter. They focus assistance at the regional/local level and are staffed by field consultants with strong sectoral expertise. Although their operating support is provided jointly by the national government (through the National Industrial Board) and regional governments (through the twenty-four County Councils), actual business services are provided by private consultants and the quasi-private Swedish Trade Council. The RDFs provide SMEs access to strategic development assistance such as technology development, high-risk financing, and business counseling—services that, according to Lars Hagg-mark, first secretary of Sweden's Ministry of Industry, "simply are not offered to SMEs by the private sector." [17] A small firm can approach its local RDF, gain information and access to a variety of national programs as well as chamber of commerce services, and receive an initial expert consultation free of charge. Subsequent services—including market analyses, product development and design services, export strategy development (including the services of an Export-Manager-for-Hire)—are fee based (see chapter 6).

The RDFs are also critical to national organizations, providing a source of feedback and an early warning system on emerging issues and needs. Says the Swedish Trade Council's Göran Sjöberg, "the RDFs are our eyes and ears at the local level."[18] In addition, according to Dr. Benny Hjern of the Swedish Council for Research in the Social Sciences and Humanities, "the RDFs create the conditions for regional variation and creativity in the delivery of public development assistance that would not be possible at the national level"[19]

# Chapter 6

# How Export Assistance Should Be Financed

*A few miles east of the chaotic heart of Rome, on one line of its rudimentary subway system, is the sprawling gray suburb of Eur. At the center of Eur is a sprawling gray campus of stark Euro-modern government office buildings, one of which houses ICE, Italy's Institute for Foreign Trade. With more than 2,000 employees distributed among its headquarters, 38 local offices throughout Italy, 78 Italian Trade Commission offices around the world, and 5 World Trade Centers in London, Paris, Tokyo, New York, and Düsseldorf, ICE is Italy's principal export promotion agency.*

*For years, ICE has offered a wide range of subsidized programs and incentives to encourage Italian firms to export: trade shows and exhibitions, trade missions, Italian product "image" promotions, market studies and market penetration consultancies, training programs for export managers, and programs to connect producers with overseas representatives. Among European industrial nations, Italy traditionally has been second only to Britain in committing public resources to promote and support export market development.*

*Now all that has changed, and the uncertainty and trepidation in the long corridors of ICE's headquarters are palpable. In March 1989, the Italian government passed Reform Law 106, requiring ICE to phase out its subsidies and charge market-rate fees for its services. Says Adele Massi of the External Relations Division, "Many people here are afraid that there is no real demand for our services and that we do not offer the services for which a market does exist."*

*Suddenly, ICE finds itself in direct competition with banks, chambers of commerce, and private consultants with substantial expertise in the nuts and bolts of export market development (as distinct from promotion). What ICE does and who it can afford to employ now depends on whether customers are willing to pay for the services it offers. The outcome is far from clear.*

79

*"It will take perhaps a year to change our regulations for the new law,"* *Massi says, "but changing the mentality of ICE will take much longer."*[1]

## No More Free Lunches

Companies must take responsibility for export market development themselves; our help is really just help at the margins.
*Brendan Doyle, Overseas Trade Division, British Overseas Trade Board*

For years many European countries have approached the problem of encouraging the growth of small- and medium-sized enterprises (SMEs) by offering direct grant subsidies in a variety of guises. Ubiquitous in the Scandinavian social democracies, the grant mentality also permeates Italy, France, and even Britain, where, after more than a decade of conservative government, program administrators still report that the most common business inquiry concerns the availability of grant assistance.

Increasingly, however, Europe and Scandinavia are abandoning direct financial subsidies in favor of fee-for-service programs, indirect subsidies, soft loans, and matching fund schemes. Tight national budgets and the prospect of slow economic growth in the 1990s have created a fiscal imperative for reducing grant assistance, but the policy motivation behind the shift is much more fundamental.

The Europeans have concluded that direct business subsidies simply do not work. Subsidies do not improve competitiveness because they do not change capabilities. They do not engender commitment to a course of action because recipients have made no meaningful investment and stand to lose little. And they do not provide public program managers with useful information on the needs of clients, because there is no market feedback, no market test for the assistance.

PUBLIC-PRIVATE POWER-SHARING AND PROGRAM FUNDING. The three countries that had perhaps the most comprehensive direct SME subsidy programs—Italy, France, and Britain—have each undergone a fundamental shift of power away from the center and toward regional governments, in much the same way that, in the United States, the government has transferred responsibilities (though not resources) to the states.

The growth in the power of Italy's regional governments, for example, has been substantial. But because the regions are largely prohibited from providing direct subsidies to businesses,[2] several—notably Emilia-Romagna, Tuscany, Lombardy, and Veneto—have created SME development and export assistance programs jointly financed by government and industry. Most are expected to become self-supporting.

In the same manner, the Mitterand government in 1982 shifted substantial economic development authority from the central government to France's regional councils. But the resources provided by the central government did not, and perhaps never could, meet the demands of the development task the regions faced. Again, the result has been a new generation of development initiatives jointly funded by the government and private sector, including the chambers of commerce and independent organizations like MIRCEB, that charge near-market fees for the services they provide.

In Britain, the shift from the center to the regions has also become a shift from the public to the private sector. Prime Minister John Major has continued Margaret Thatcher's policy of privatization, transferring a wide range of public services to local "enterprise agencies" governed by boards of directors composed of local businesspeople and regional representatives of central government. The government has assigned the delivery of some export assistance services to branches of the Association of British Chambers of Commerce (ABCC) and, through assisted consultancies, to private sector experts. Even so, the regional offices of the Department of Trade and

Industry, which administers the British Overseas Trade Board (BOTB), continue to be the first point of contact on export questions.


FROM FINANCIAL INDUCEMENTS TO SERVICI REALI. While a direct subsidy for exporting may reduce a product's final price in the international marketplace and make the product more competitive, it does nothing to improve the competitiveness of the producer. Either the subsidy must continue indefinitely or the firm's export ventures will falter and eventually fail. Italy's answer to the subsidy cycle is *servici reali*—"real services." Real services are those that improve the production quality or efficiency of the firm, differentiate its products from others, or help reach or redefine a market.[3]

While the concept originated in northern and central Italy, the provision of real services has become a central feature of most European export assistance programs for SMEs. The Swedish Trade Council, for example, describes the jointly funded, fee-for-service export assistance programs it offers Swedish SMEs as "help towards self-help."[4] Norman Arends, MIRCEB's vice president for North American Operations, characterizes the services his organization provides to Brittany's SMEs as designed "to help our companies go further, faster."[5] Virtually identical phrases are used by public and private program administrators throughout Europe. The focus of investment is on strengthening firms through management development, technology deployment and product development, market analysis, training, and the brokering of specific export deals that lead to long-term trade relationships. Governments that provide public funds to support real services generally require a contribution from the private sector, provide loans instead of grants, and increasingly require firms receiving services to pay fees, though often below market rates. The objective is to get firms to stand on their own rather than to prop them up in the international marketplace.

THE COST OF COMMITMENT. Finally, virtually all of the services offered by the best export assistance programs, whether public, private, or quasi-private, are now fee based. As Philippe Houchois, former manager of MIRCEB's Seattle office, has testified before the Oregon legislature, "Charging companies [a fee] is a way of ensuring the commitment of those companies. Because experience has shown that free services are not valued the way they should be. . . . [We] think that asking for a financial contribution is a way of committing the company to the project in the same way that we commit to work on that project."[6]

## Lesson 10:  *Exporting is worthwhile only if it is profitable; if it is profitable, assistance should be paid for.*

Fees are the acid test of market demand.
*Richard Riley, Export Promotion Policy Unit, British Overseas Trade Board*

If a company can't pay the fee, it shouldn't be in the market.
*Dr. Armin Grünewald, Association of German Chambers of Industry and Commerce*

The practice now common in Europe of requiring SMEs to pay for export services, even if those services are partly subsidized, is a form of triage, not unlike the practice of providing export assistance only to those firms that can demonstrate their export-readiness. Requiring payment screens out those dabbling in export markets and, at the same time, ensures a level of commitment that grants or other direct financial inducements fail to ensure.

Program administrators disagree about how much resistance they can expect to paying fees for services—especially services that formerly were free. Tell Hermanson, head of the

International Relations department of the Stockholm Chamber of Commerce, notes, "Small entrepreneurial companies are used to paying for raw materials and hard products, but not for services and time; it is a learning process."[7] Officials in northern Italy report that, despite the success of sectoral service centers, getting small artisanal firms to pay even nominal fees is an uphill battle. In 1989, after two years of operation, RESFOR had only 600 paid members from a pool of 16,000 small metalworking firms in Emilia-Romagna.[8] The director of SVEX, Emilia-Romagna's service center for export development, estimated that, even after a year, he spent 80 percent of his time on the phone encouraging firms to become paying members.[9] In Germany export development is predominantly a private sector activity, but there too some resistance is acknowledged. Gunter Kayser of Germany's Institute for Research on Medium-Sized Firms comments, "SMEs have to learn to pay for information—to handle information the same as human capital."[10]

Despite fears to the contrary, organizations that have switched from free to fee-based services, or that have substantially raised existing fees to market or near-market levels, have experienced little or no drop-off in demand. Howard Gladwell of the Birmingham office of Britain's Department of Trade and Industry reports that the agency has not only exceeded its targets for chargeable fees (although the targets have been raised repeatedly) but improved the quality of its services as well, reflecting the higher expectations generated by the fee system.[11] Other European agencies have similar stories to tell. The chamber of commerce of Rennes, France (in Brittany), which had already covered half its operating costs through service fees, raised its fees recently in order to provide expanded services. To its surprise, the chamber has found that its customers now value the services more, in part because they have improved—but also, the chamber thinks, because they cost more.[12]

Requiring both fees and significant private sector financial commitments in export assistance programs is now common throughout Europe. In Germany, which has perhaps the most market-driven export assistance system, the Foreign Trade Institute of North Rhine-Westphalia is adamant about fees. "It is absolutely necessary for firms to bear most of the cost," according to Managing Director Helga Massow—if only to ensure that they take the task before them seriously.[13] Sweden's image as a welfare state notwithstanding, its Trade Council has always charged for export assistance services: below market rates for members, higher fees for nonmembers. Initiatives such as the Export Manager-for-Hire program are explicitly designed to phase out financial support quickly and place full financial responsibility on the company. And even the recently scrapped export market development programs of Denmark's National Agency of Industry and Trade required substantial private matching funds, offering public sector support in the form of soft loans repayable as firms began to generate export business and forgivable only in the event of failure. Denmark's new network program requires participating groups of firms to provide a 50 percent match to cover operating costs.[14]

However, the shift to fees and substantial private sector financial participation has not meant the abdication of public sector responsibility for export market development in any of the European nations. In fact, while private sector involvement is clearly on the rise, only in Germany is it likely that the private and quasi-private initiatives profiled earlier would have emerged without prodding from a public sector acting on behalf of firms too small to be of interest to private service providers. SMEs are of interest only to their owners and employees and to governments that see in these firms the potential for economic growth and expanded opportunities. In a market economy, banks, export consultants, major accounting firms, trading companies, and other large enterprises cannot be faulted for showing little interest in export deals so small that the transaction costs outweigh profits. And small firms cannot be faulted for avoiding export markets so fraught with risks that, without assistance, novice exporters risk financial ruin. The potential is obvious, but so are the risks. In all the innovative programs explored here, government's role is to represent the collective interest of society and, by creating market-failure-correcting incentives, to bridge the yawning gap between risk and potential reward.

## PROGRAM PROFILE
*Britain's Export Service Card and Quality Management System*

Few nations have done a better job of making export assistance services more accessible to small firms than Britain. The Export Initiative, part of a nationwide Enterprise Initiative aimed at strengthening SMEs' contributions to economic growth, restructured a disparate array of export-related services into a single coherent strategy. This strategy was communicated to businesses around the nation through a variety of media, including a well-designed family of publications aimed at explaining how to begin exporting and use specific services at specific stages in the export development process. Private sector players became directly involved in the delivery of some services, and local and regional offices, more accessible to their customers, were given responsibility for the actual delivery of services. In 1992, a further restructuring integrated the export promotion activities of the Department of Trade and Industry (through the British Overseas Trade Board), the Foreign and Commonwealth Office, and the industrial development divisions of the Scottish, Welsh, and Northern Ireland Offices, under a single management directorate. The Export Initiative marketing banner was changed to Overseas Trade Services to reflect the change and simplify points of contact and service delivery procedures.

The department recognized that if fees were to be raised and new charges assessed, customers would participate only if it was convenient and if they felt they were getting value for their money. As the BOTB's 1990-91 business plan notes, "Businessmen who are seriously involved in securing export business will not be deterred by the existence of reasonable charges [for BOTB services]. Equally, it is clear that they are not prepared to pay for services that do not meet their need for accuracy, reliability, and timeliness."[15]

Convenience was improved by the creation of a service card. The card operates much like an American Express card, allowing customers to charge services provided by Overseas Trade Services in London, local and regional offices, and overseas; services can even be ordered by phone. While the card does not offer credit, it does enable businesses to buy help and defer payment until the end of the month, when they are billed by the Service Card Center. The card also simplifies the customer's record-keeping and allows the board to communicate more easily with customers. Moreover, it reinforces the coherence of the nation's export assistance program every time it is used. While customers are pleased with the convenience of the card, its administration has proved somewhat unwieldy; in mid-1992, the program was under review and expected to be modified, though not abandoned.

Finally, Britain has instituted a Quality Management System to sample customer satisfaction on the full range of export services offered by the department and its private sector partners every month. Though the system is too new to have had much effect on programs and services, it demonstrates that administrators and private service providers are expected to make a good showing or face restructuring or cancellation of contracts.

*Chapter 7*

# Conclusion: Thinking Strategically about Export Assistance

The United States has been slow to recognize the strategic importance of a coherent and aggressive export policy. During the last twenty-five years, as the world economy splintered into niches and competition globalized, the federal government has taken an active interest in export promotion only sporadically, and then primarily as a response to deficits, not as part of an explicit growth strategy.[1] More recently, the U.S. Department of Commerce has sought to encourage small- and medium-sized firms (SMEs) to become exporters, but with little visible success. The Reagan administration exhorted firms to export, yet pursued trade and monetary policies—such as permitting the dollar to soar against other currencies—that effectively precluded export expansion.

## America's Underdeveloped Export Infrastructure

> Unfortunately, the export fabric of the United States, which has never been strong, largely disintegrated in the mid-1980s.[2]
> *William Krist, President, American Electronics Association*

As the 1980s ended, the federal government's policymakers were occupied with the nation's trade disputes with Japan and the problem of agricultural subsidies in the Uruguay round of the General Agreement on Trade and Tariffs (GATT) negotiations. Relatively little attention was given to developing an effective export infrastructure to support the nation's SMEs. Then, in 1990, the U.S. and Foreign Commercial Service (US&FCS, the government's principal export assistance outreach arm) developed a new strategic plan designed, according to Director General Susan Schwab, to "focus our energies primarily on small- and medium-sized firms with limited export experience and capability—infrequent exporters—and established exporters that are trying to penetrate a new market."[3]

This is an important step, and one that is consistent with the lessons learned by the Europeans about targeting assistance where it is most effective. In 1992 the U.S. General Accounting Office reported that ten executive branch agencies spent $2.7 billion on export promotion but that their activities were not guided by any explicit strategy or set of priorities. Indeed three-quarters of all federal export promotion spending was for agricultural exports, which represent only about 10 percent of the value of all U.S. exports. A third of these agricultural export promotion funds went to very large, well-established exporters fully capable of paying for their own export market development activities.[4]

It is unclear whether the federal government has either the will or the resources to deliver the tangible assistance services SMEs require. The performance of the private sector is no better. The nation's chambers of commerce and many trade associations are neither equipped nor, apparently, motivated to provide the range of professional export services offered by their European counterparts. Meanwhile, as they have in other areas of microeconomic policy, the states have stepped in to provide the export assistance services the federal government and private sector have failed to provide.

## The Rise of the Trading State

> Who's going to do it if the states don't? The feds won't, the banks don't, and the trade associations haven't yet.
> *Herb Ouida, Director, XPORT, Port Authority of New York and New Jersey*

Begun as early as the 1950s, state international trade programs initially focused on recruiting foreign investment, not on developing or promoting exports by in-state manufacturers.[5] The balance began to shift, however, after the 1981-82 reces-

Table 7-1. *State International Trade Activities*

| | |
|---|---|
| Overseas offices | Catalogue shows |
| Trade shows | Counseling/technical assistance |
| Recruiting foreign investment | Export service referrals |
| Trade leads | Visiting buyer assistance |
| Seminars/workshops/conferences | Foreign trade zones |
| Sector/country targeting | Export trading companies |
| Trade finance/insurance | Honorary ambassadors/attaches |
| Exporter awards | Joint venture matching |
| Sister-State programs | Newsletters/export handbooks |
| Language banks | Trade statistics |
| Market studies | Export product directories |
| Exporter directories | Directories of agents and distributors |
| Trade missions | |

Source: Blaine Liner, "States and Localities in the Global Marketplace," *Intergovernmental Perspective*, vol. 16 (Spring 1990), p. 12.

sion, when state trade programs expanded rapidly, adding services such as trade lead data collection and dissemination, market research, trade fair and trade mission promotion and assistance, export counseling, seminars, publications, and overseas trade offices, among other services (see table 7-1). By 1990, according to the National Association of State Development Agencies, states were spending more than $90 million annually on international economic development activities, including both export promotion and foreign investment recruitment, more than four times what they had spent only six years earlier.[6] The actual dollar amounts range from as much as 20 percent of a state's total economic development budget to as little as 1 percent, or even less.[7]

Overseas trade offices have multiplied. In 1984, 27 states had 52 overseas offices in 10 countries[8]; by 1989, 44 states had 158 offices in 27 countries.[9] By 1990 the total number of state foreign offices had risen to 163 and the cost of running them had reached $33 million—fully one-third of total state international spending.[10] Gubernatorial trade missions have been another boom industry: a National Governors' Association survey found that forty-one governors had made eighty-two trips to thirty-five countries in 1989 to promote trade, though most of these trips were designed to attract foreign investment.[11]

As state export assistance programs have increased in scale and sophistication, they have begun to influence federal policy as well. The U.S. Commerce Department is working closely with a number of states to coordinate export promotion techniques and trade data. As a result of a pilot program begun in 1986, the US&FCS's 129 district offices are now working with state trade programs to improve information sharing, cooperative planning, and joint trade initiatives. And as of 1992 the Eximbank had two cities and nineteen states in its City-State Program, designed to bring the bank's services closer to small exporters. [12]

Yet despite this explosion of state-led export promotion activities and the federal government's eagerness to jump on the state bandwagon, few programs have been evaluated for their wisdom and effectiveness. Those reviews that have been conducted are less than complimentary.

—A review of state assistance to exporters conducted by the Michigan Department of Commerce found, "Many states have invested considerable resources in this area, and to date most of these programs are wallowing or failing." [13]

—An Urban Institute analyst recently reported, "Often . . . international programs are provided mostly because other states have them." [14]

—An assessment of the National Association of State Development Agencies' 1990 survey of state export expenditures concluded, "Observers can draw two major conclusions from these numbers. One is that most states do not appear to spend much to promote exports. Second, most states are unprepared—even unwilling—to identify their total spending on international functions." [15]

—A Hubert H. Humphrey Institute of Public Affairs evaluation of state international programs concluded that "an incomplete understanding of the impact of expenditures in one's own state and in others may be leading to quite a bit of 'shooting in the dark'." [16]

—A study commissioned by the U.S. Small Business Administration found that, "Not only is it not possible to relate state export promotion activity to overall state exports, it is not possible to relate state export promotion activity to exports by those very firms which had been helped."[17]

If it is unclear what state export assistance programs are accomplishing, part of the reason is that it is unclear what, in a strategic sense, they hope to accomplish. Almost without exception, state export promotion programs target SMEs, especially manufacturers. In most states, there is little additional targeting, except in the case of sector-specific trade shows. The states try to make businesses more aware of the benefits of exporting, expose firms to export opportunities (through trade leads, missions, and the like), and promote their state's products and producers abroad.

But research suggests that few states have a clear sense of what these firms need or organize export assistance services to address those needs. The Urban Institute, for example, did a statistical analysis of export assistance programs in Illinois, which has a very large export promotion budget, and found virtually no difference between the export performance of firms that used state assistance and those that did not. The study concluded that the state had done little to understand the needs of the firms it hoped to help. Another assessment, this one of both state and federal export promotion programs, concluded that many appear to have been created without clear long-term goals, lack specific and thus measurable objectives, fail to target client groups carefully, do not appear to be driven by felt needs. These overlapping programs, delivered by agencies lacking credibility with businesses, fail to incorporate the lessons of past experience and benefit from little or no evaluation of their effectiveness. The researchers concluded, "Often, 'high-profile' activities have prevailed over the high-yield activities."[18]

## Adoption versus Adaptation: Learning from Europe

With their small domestic economies, the Europeans have had little choice but to struggle to create high-yield export market development programs for SMEs. Some of these programs are time tested and effective; others are new but intriguing. But transatlantic program-swapping is fraught with difficulties. For one thing, there is a tradition of government intervention in private economic affairs in Europe that has never made the crossing to the New World. The public sector in Europe is large and, whether the government in power is conservative, socialist, or social democratic, generally takes a more active role in managing economic transitions than is the case in the United States.[19] As U.S. Representative Andy Ireland noted at a recent congressional hearing on SME export problems, "In most other countries of the world, when small businesses decide to export, one of the first places they go for assistance is their own government."[20]

But the congressman is only half right. Certainly the public sector plays a more active part in export assistance in most European countries than it does in the United States. But the private sector generally plays an even stronger part—again, a much stronger part than it plays in the United States. European businesses and the organizations representing them exhibit a commitment to long-term thinking, experimenting, evaluating, and investing in the basic resources required for business growth that is seldom evident in the United States. The well-developed private sector infrastructure is specifically designed to provide concrete assistance to SMEs that want to go global. Moreover, Europe has a long tradition of cooperation between government, business, and labor unions. While conflicts can and do arise on such issues as wages or taxes, the "social partners" work closely together to analyze and resolve economic policy matters. And export market development is one area in which private and public sector cooperation is strong.

## Conclusion

Given these differences, what conclusions can Americans draw from the experiences of Europe's best SME export assistance programs?

Ironically, the most important conclusion may well be to ignore Europe's programs and focus instead on the principles they embody. Programs are often culture specific; principles transcend cultures. None of the programs profiled here has solved the SME export problem to the complete satisfaction of either those who administer them or those who use them. Precisely how the Europeans help smaller firms export matters less than understanding the principles that underlie what they do and why they do it.

From the ten lessons explored in the preceding chapters, five broad conclusions emerge that can guide state, private, and even federal policymakers as the United States struggles to help its SMEs compete in the global economy.

*Everyone wants to increase small firms' exports, and everyone finds it difficult.*

No one concerned with economic development, on either side of the Atlantic, has failed to grasp the potential many SMEs have for export growth. But these firms are hard to reach and hard to help. Because of their size, and sometimes their youth, they tend to be fragile. Small hurdles can become insurmountable barriers, small setbacks can be fatal.

Many European export assistance program officials will admit that even their most successful initiatives operate at the margins. In any given year, these programs provide only a few firms with limited assistance. Yet most officials believe that this marginal difference makes a difference. And while they complain that too few small firms export, the export performance of SMEs in most European countries is much higher than it is in the United States. The Europeans' deep sense of urgency about export trade, evident in both public and private sectors, stands in sharp contrast to attitudes in the United States. The new competitive pressure the integration of the European market will create is certainly one source of this urgency. But Europeans see beyond that immediate challenge and view SME exporting as an essential component of global competitiveness.

This does not mean, however, that the Europeans have found the solution to generating SME export growth. They are still searching for a solution—or, to be more accurate, many solutions—to the problem of increasing the global competitiveness of their smaller firms. They keep revising established programs and inventing new ones to respond to changes in both the global marketplace and the needs of SMEs. In general, Europeans are hard at work on the problem; the same cannot be said for most Americans.

*Targeting is crucial.*

The European experience suggests that national export assistance programs, whether public or private, tend to be too general to be effective for SMEs. The needs of these firms are too varied and the conditions under which they must compete too uncertain for large-scale, centrally administered programs to work. To a substantial extent, both the emerging trend toward down-sizing Europe's large-scale national export assistance programs by targeting specific regions and sectors and the increasing customization of export assistance services are responses to dissatisfaction with the assistance delivered through nationwide programs. In countries where this process has not occurred, local organizations are emerging to provide the customized services national programs do not provide.

There are advantages to starting or becoming small and focusing on a specific clientele. Trade development happens one deal at a time. The export assistance programs that appear the most promising are those designed to help identify and broker individual deals. The problem with deep, specific, customized export assistance services, of course, is that no organization—public, private, or jointly sponsored—can afford to provide such services to many firms, given limited budgets. This fiscal fact of life is one reason why fee-based services are growing rapidly. Local and regional initiatives in Europe suggest that carefully targeted, modestly funded trade development programs can, despite their smallness, generate enough success to move other firms to "buy in." Though it is too soon to say with certainty, officials heading these small-scale programs in some parts of Europe anticipate that successful firms will form networks to support each other and the export services they value so that the export assistance programs become self-sustaining.

*Focus available resources on those firms that will help themselves.*

Virtually no one in Europe spends much time trying to turn the export oblivious into the export willing. Along with the trend toward fee-based services, activities are designed to eliminate less serious exporters and focus on those firms, both new and established, that have both sufficient management maturity to develop competent strategic plans and the resources to make a financial commitment to export market development.

The best corollary to the export willing in the United States is what the US&FCS and some states call "infrequent exporters"—firms that have shown some interest in exporting and have the potential for more, if only they can obtain the necessary assistance. The challenge facing those who want to help them is to identify which firms within this surprisingly large group have the managerial depth and financial where-withal to undertake more frequent export activity.

If there is a weakness to this strategy, it is that some, and perhaps many, of these firms will begin exporting or expand their exporting business without assistance. The solution to this problem lies in requiring firms to make a substantial investment. As states, private organizations, and the federal government struggle to provide tangible export assistance services despite limited or declining budgets, developing the kinds of services such firms will be willing to pay for is the crucial first step toward creating high-yield exporting.

*Creating world-class international trade programs requires understanding the difference between export promotion and export market development.*

Export promotion programs that create awareness of exporting as an option for economic growth and business expansion, offer incentives to persuade firms to export, and sponsor trade missions, trade shows, and other promotional events high-lighting products have been the staples of federal, state, and industry-run export trade programs in the United States for years. But promotion—hawking products abroad—is essentially a one-way street. It is supply driven and episodic, providing companies with relatively little intelligence they can use to identify and penetrate new markets. Either promotional programs result in sales or they do not; companies seldom have any idea why and are the poorer as a result.

Market development, on the other hand—the process of identifying or creating emerging markets or market niches and modifying products to penetrate those markets—is a two-way street. It is demand driven rather than supply driven and is the preferred method of creating long-term export capacity. But it is nearly impossible for small firms to acquire market intelligence—which takes time and costs money—on their own, for few small firms have these commodities in quantity.

What distinguishes many of the most imaginative export assistance programs developed in Europe from most federal, state, and private sector export programs in the United States is their focus on market development. The European programs help firms anticipate, identify, respond to, or create, overseas markets not just for an existing product, but for future products. These nations also participate in trade promotion programs, often quite aggressively, but they do not pretend that these activities are a substitute for real market development.

*Just as exporting must be part of a company's overall strategic plan for growth, export development must be part of a state's or a nation's overall economic competitiveness strategy.*

Perhaps the most troubling thing about many of Europe's SME export assistance programs is how well they are integrated into a broad and coherent national strategy for establishing or maintaining competitiveness in the global marketplace. Indeed, many European officials resist the idea of separating export policy from policies on technology, training, and education, among other economic cornerstones. The United Kingdom's Export Initiative, for example, is really a subpart of a much broader Enterprise Initiative. Denmark's export network program is only one part of an ambitious effort to upgrade the technical and managerial sophistication of even the smallest firms. Germany's trade programs are connected to a range of social and economic programs designed to strengthen the Mittelstand, the SMEs that are the backbone of that country's economy. In Lombardy and Emilia-Romagna, two of northern Italy's strongest regions economically, export market development is simply one part of a comprehensive program to help small, often family-owned, businesses compete with the world's largest corporations.

The United States, in contrast, is beset by discrete issues and seems incapable of addressing them as parts of a coherent economic strategy. This is true both at the federal level and among the trade associations and other business organizations that seek to influence federal policy. It is somewhat less true at the state level. With the steady devolution of responsibility for many economic activities from the federal to state government and the continuous pressure to create jobs, income, and revenue, some states have begun to understand that export market development, technology development and deployment, and workforce competence are components of a larger challenge: creating a coherent economic development strategy. It makes little sense to create sophisticated international trade programs if the products to be traded do not meet international standards for quality and technological sophistication. Similarly, it makes little sense to try to upgrade technology in SMEs if their employees lack the skills to work with that technology. The issues are not separable.

Similarly, within the context of export trade development itself, it makes little sense to spend public or private dollars on export promotion when sellers and buyers who become motivated to trade as a result of that promotion discover there is no infrastructure to make trade possible. Unlike many of its competitors, the United States does not have a well-developed network of trade facilitation services. The inadequacy of its trade infrastructure is most glaring in the field of export finance, but the absence of export-minded trade associations capable of providing concrete assistance to firms, the lack of affordable and accessible market data services, and difficulty in acquiring assistance on product standards, among other things, sharply limit the competitiveness of the United States' SME exporters. No business, no matter how highly motivated, can succeed in the international marketplace without the same kind of trade infrastructure support its competitors are receiving.

## A Note

In August 1991, Dun and Bradstreet published its annual export outlook survey for 1991 and 1992. The survey used a 5,000-firm sample, selected and weighted so that it was statistically representative of all U.S. businesses. The outlook was not good.

In terms of volume, over 50 percent of all growth in the U.S. economy since 1986 can be attributed to gains in exports. In 1990, exports accounted for over 90 percent of economic growth.[21] Clearly, export growth is crucial to the nation's future. But the 1991 Dun's survey found that only about 50 percent of the firms surveyed expect to increase imports in 1992—down from 64 percent in 1990. Moreover, the proportion of firms that export also declined. Finally, only 1 percent of firms that did not export in 1991 had any plans to do so in 1992, a drop of more than 50 percent from the previous year.[22]

These declining expectations could be interpreted as fall-out from the 1991 recession. But the firms reported that structural barriers, such as the availability of trade lead data and export financing, were at least as important as world economic conditions in limiting their export expectations.

In short, America's future economic growth is hamstrung not by global economic factors beyond its control but by tangible structural barriers within its control that keep firms, including those that have exported in the past, from even entering export markets, much less competing successfully in them.

The message from Europe is simple: while these countries have not devised a perfect formula for helping SMEs go global, they are at least working on it. There is little evidence the United States is doing the same.

# NOTES

## Chapter 1

1. According to a 1990 census commissioned by the London Docklands Development Corporation, 95 percent of all Docklands businesses employed fewer than one hundred people, and 62 percent employed fewer than ten, although just over one-half of all employees work in larger firms with more than one hundred employees. More than half of all businesses were start-ups.

2. All data derived from International Monetary Fund, *International Financial Statistics April 1991* (Washington, 1991).

3. Informal testimony before the Subcommittee on Exports, Tax Policy, and Special Problems of the House Committee on Small Business, March 1991.

4. Informal testimony, March 1991.

5. Informal testimony, March 1991.

6. Testimony of J. Michael Farren, under secretary for international trade, U.S. Department of Commerce, in *Export Trade Promotion Programs, Federal and Private Sector Roles*, Hearing before the Subcommittee on International Economic Policy and Trade of the House Committee on Foreign Affairs, 101 Cong. 2 sess. (Goverment Printing Office, 1991), p. 2.

7. Chris Farrell and others, "At Last, Good News," *Business Week*, June 3, 1991, p. 24.

8. C. Fred Bergsten, "Rx for America: Export-Led Growth," *International Economic Insights*, vol. 2 (January/February 1991), p. 3.

9. Quoted in John Burgess, "U.S. Trade Deficit Down to $5.3 Billion in February," *Washington Post*, April 19, 1991, p. A6.

10. According to the Institute for International Economics, "sizeable increases have been recorded in electrical equipment, specialized industrial machinery such as forklift trucks and compressors, telecommunications products, photographic and optical equipment, computers, and scientific instruments. There have been impressive gains in such 'surprise' sectors as furniture, textile yarn, apparel, auto parts, musical instruments, and

minivans as well as traditional sources of strength such as aircraft and chemicals." Bergsten, "Rx for America," pp. 3–4.

11. Sylvia Nasar, "Boom in Manufactured Exports Provides Hope for U.S. Economy," *New York Times*, April 21, 1991, p. A22.

12. Industrial Technology Institute, "Base Modernization: The Opportunity," *TechnEcon*, vol. 1 (Spring 1989), p. 4; and "Industrial Base Modernization: An American Priority," *TechnEcon*, vol. 2 (Summer 1990), pp. 1–4.

13. Bergsten, "Rx for America," p. 5.

14. Interview with Michael Farrell, Foreign Trade Division, Bureau of the Census, U.S. Department of Commerce, December 1991.

15. The Census Bureau distinguishes between enterprises and firms. Their statistics do not include the 10.9 million "mom and pop" firms without paid employees. Nor do they include agriculture, forestry, and fisheries businesses; finance, insurance, and real estate businesses, and certain categories of service businesses.

16. Bureau of the Census, *1987 Enterprise Statistics, ES87-3 Company Summary* (Department of Commerce, 1991); and unpublished analyses by the Data Analysis and Planning Staff, Foreign Trade Division, Bureau of the Census, 1991.

17. Data derived by matching Shipper's Export Declarations with Bureau of the Census, *1987 Enterprise Statistics*.

18. Unpublished analysis by Leslie Stroh, editor and publisher, *The Exporter*, Trade Data Reports, Inc., New York.

19. Interview with Leslie Stroh, editor and publisher, *The Exporter*, 1991.

20. U.S. General Accounting Office, National Security and International Affairs Division, *Export Promotion: Federal Programs Lack Organization and Funding Cohesiveness* (Washington, January 1992), p. 6.

21. Bureau of the Census, *1987 Enterprise Statistics*, p. 14.

22. In a number of countries, the smallest companies still complain that larger firms dominate the political agenda, but it seems a matter of degree, and small firms have strong representative organizations in many countries.

## Notes to Chapter 2

1. Daniel E. Pilcher and Lanny Proffer, *The States and International Trade: New Roles in Export Development* (Denver, Colo.: National Conference of State Legislatures, 1985), p. 13.

2. S. Tamer Cavusgil and Michael R. Czinkota, *International Perspectives on Trade Promotion and Assistance* (New York: Quorum Books, 1990), p. xiii.

3. Pilcher and Proffer, *The States*.

4. Pilcher and Proffer, *The States*.

5. K. Mark Weaver, *Small Business in Export Markets* (Washington: National Federation of Independent Business, 1985), pp. 37–40.

6. S. Tamer Cavusgil, "Public Policy Implications of Research on the Export Behavior of Firms," *Akron Business and Economic Review*, vol. 14 (Summer 1983), p. 17.

7. Graham Bannock and Partners, *Into Active Exporting* (London: British Overseas Trade Board, 1987), p. 27.

8. European Commission, "The Participation of Small and Medium-Sized Enterprise in Exporting Outside the Community," vol. 1: Main Report—Summary and Recommendations, Netherlands, January 1989, p. 27.

9. Interview with Martin F. Parnell, Liverpool Business School, November 1990.

10. Interview with John Endean, American Business Conference, Washington, 1991.

11. Interview with Adele Massi, Istituto Nazionale per il Commercio Estero, Rome, December 1989.

12. Interview with Michele Simonin, Chambre de Commerce et d'Industrie de Paris, November 1990.

13. Interview with Gunter Kayser, Institut für Mittelstandforschung, Bonn, November 1990.

14. Lawrence S. Welch and Finn Wiedersheim-Paul, "Initial Exports—A Marketing Failure?" cited in F. H. Rolf Seringhaus and Philip J. Rosson, *Government Export Promotion: A Global Perspective* (Routledge, 1990), p. 172.

15. Interview with Göran Sjöberg, Swedish Trade Council, Stockholm, December 1989.

16. Interview with Kent Goldmann, Swedish Trade Council, Stockholm, December 1989.

17. Interview with Stefan Wengler, Department of International Market Policy, Federation of German Industries, Cologne, November 1990.

18. Interview with Poul Breum, Danish Technology Institute, Aarhus, December 1989.

19. Breum, interview, December 1989.

## Notes to Chapter 3

1. Interview with Peter Bishop, London Chamber of Commerce and Industry, London, November 1990.

2. London Chamber of Commerce and Industry, brochure, *London Chamber Export Now*, 1990.

3. Based on a conversion rate of 1.7 U.S. dollars to the pound sterling.

4. Based on a conversion rate of DM 1.83 to the U.S. dollar.

5. Interview with Johannes Olesen Larsen, Ministry of Industry, Denmark, December 1989.

6. European Commission, "The Participation of Small-and Medium-Sized Enterprises in Exporting Outside the Community," vol. 1: Main Report—Summary and Recommendations," Netherlands, January 1989, p. 16.

7. U.S. Department of Commerce, "Export Promotion Activities of Major Competitor Nations," p. 20; and unpublished analysis of the Mediocredito data base, Bocconi University, Milan, 1989.

8. Tom Peters, "The German Economic Miracle Nobody Knows," *Across the Board*, vol. 27 (April 1990), p. 20.

9. The other two are Baden-Wurttemberg and Bavaria.

10. Gordon McRoberts and Carol Conway, "Wholesalers and Retailers of Export Assistance: The State-Local Roles of the Future?" *Local Insight No. 10* (Southern Growth Policies Board, Research Triangle Park, February 1990), p. 1.

11. National Association of State Development Agencies (NASDA), "Introduction and Analysis of 1990 SEPD Data" (Washington, 1991), pp. 30–31.

12. Michigan Department of Commerce, "Trends in State Export Promotion Strategies," Lansing, 1989.

13. U.S. Department of Commerce, "Export Promotion Activities," p. 37.

14. Interview with Jens Mastrup, HK-Aarhus, Aarhus, December 1989.

15. Testimony of Leslie Stroh, editor and publisher of *The Exporter*, before the Subcommittee on Economic Policy and Foreign Trade of the House Committee on Foreign Affairs, 102 Cong. 1 sess. (Government Printing Office, 1990).

16. See, for example, C. Richard Hatch, *Flexible Manufacturing Networks: Cooperation for Competitiveness in a Global Economy* (Washington: Corporation for Enterprise Development, 1989); Joseph Cortright, *Old*

*World New Ideas: Business Assistance Lessons from Europe* (University of Washington, Northwest Policy Center, 1990); Stuart A. Rosenfeld, *Technology, Innovation, and Rural Development: Lessons from Italy and Denmark* (Washington: Aspen Institute, December 1990); and Edward Goodman and Julia Bamford, eds., *Small Firms and Industrial Districts in Italy* (Routledge, 1989).

## Notes to Chapter 4

1. Based on a conversion rate of 6.2 francs to the U.S. dollar.

2. Interview with Tell Hermanson, Stockholm Chamber of Commerce, December 1989.

3. Interview with Klaus Dornbush, German Ministry of Industry, Bonn, November 1990.

4. See, for example, European Commission, "The Participation of Small- and Medium-Sized Enterprise in Exporting Outside the Community," vol. 1: Main Report—Summary and Recommendations, Netherlands, January 1989; Graham Bannock and Partners, *Into Active Exporting* (London: British Overseas Trade Board, 1987); and Donald G. Howard and Irene M. Herremans, "Sources of Assistance for Small Business Exporters," *Journal of Small Business Management*, vol. 26 (July 1988), pp. 48–54.

5. Adapted from F. H. Rolf Seringhaus and Philip J. Rosson, *Government Export Promotion: A Global Perspective* (Routledge, 1990), p. 31.

6. For a more detailed description of the export information services provided by U.S. and European export agencies, see U.S. Department of Commerce, "Export Promotion Activities of Major Competitor Nations," July 1988.

7. U.S. Department of Commerce, International Trade Administration, U.S. and Foreign Commercial Service, "Trade Opportunities Program to Make Contacts," 1989.

8. As this was written, BC-NET was still in its trial stage. There are some 200 European Information Centres throughout the Community, each connected to Brussels by EUROKOM, an electronic mail system. The centres provide SMEs access to information on trade statistics, exporting to and from member states, business contacts, export documentation, "harmonisation" of product standards, tenders, public procurement contracts, and a range of other single market issues such as institutions and contacts, directives and regulations, grants and loans, structural funds, competition policy, and R&D programs.

9. IFT Marketing Research, *Respondent Summary Report on the Quality Management System for 1989* (London: Department of Trade and Industry and Foreign Commonwealth Office, June 1990), p. 4.

10. N. Mansfield, C. Wheeler, and S. Young, "The Use of Information for Exporting Construction Services," cited in J. Tamer Cavusgil and Michael R. Czinkota, *International Perspectives on Trade Promotion and Assistance* (New York: Quorum Books, 1990), p. 111.

11. The European Commission protested the Export Market Research Scheme as anti-competitive. The British Overseas Trade Board finessed the objection by contracting with companies for the research, rather than giving the money to them directly, and by requiring a 50 percent match.

12. Interview with Johannes Olesen Larsen, Ministry of Industry, Copenhagen, December 1989.

13. Interview with Armin Grunewald, German Association of Chambers of Industry and Commerce, Bonn, November 1990.

14. The program defines SMEs as firms with less than $50 million in annual turnover, but the average turnover of participating firms is less than $8 million.

15. COFACE, *A Guide to COFACE's Facilities* (Paris: COFACE, 1988), pp. 7–8.

16. Interview with Alain Paupert, Compagnie Francaise d'Assurance pour le Commerce Extérieur, Paris, November 1990.

17. "Financial Assistance for Export Promotion" EUROLOC Database, EPRC Limited, in association with the University of Strathclyde, Glasgow, Scotland.

18. Centre Francais du Commerce Exterieur and Comite Francais de Manifestations Economiques a l'Etranger, "Activities 1989 En Quelques Chiffres," Paris, 1990.

19. COFACE, *Guide to Facilities*, pp. 8–9.

20. British Overseas Trade Board (BOTB), *Report 1989/1990* (London: Department of Trade and Industry, 1990), pp. 30–34.

21. BOTB, *Specific Export Help* (London: Department of Trade and Industry, 1990), pp. 13–14.

22. Ausstellungs-und Messe-Ausschuss der Deutschen Wirtschaft (AUMA), *AUMA Report '89*, July 1990, p. 3.

23. Interview with Margarete Hentschel, Foreign Trade Fairs Division, AUMA, November 1990.

24. AUMA, *Report*, p. 6.

25. Interview with Helga Massow, Foreign Trade Promotion Institute, North Rhine-Westphalia, November 1990.

26. Carl Arthur Solberg, "Export Promotion and Trade Fairs in Norway: Are There Better Ways?" in Cavusgil and Czinkota, *International Perspectives*, p. 121.

27. BOTB, *Report 1989/1990*, p. 33.

28. National Association of State Development Agencies (NASDA), "Introduction and Analysis of 1990 SEPD Data" (Washington, 1991), pp. 39, 41.

29. Solberg, "Export Promotion," p. 122.

30. Hentschel, interview, November 1990.

31. Massow, interview, November 1990.

32. Marlene M. Morales, "The X-PORT Port Authority Trading Company: An Innovative Approach to Export Development," cited in Washington State Senate Economic Development and Labor Committee, Seattle, by Senator Emilio Cantu, *Pacific Northwest Export Assistance Center, A Proposal*, November 1990, p. 20.

33. Leslie Stroh, Testimony before the Subcommittee on Economic Policy and Foreign Trade of the House Committee on Foreign Affairs, 102 Cong. 1 sess. (Government Printing Office, 1990).

34. Alex F. De Noble and Michael J. Belch, "The Intermediary Needs of Domestic Exporters: An Empirical Analysis," cited in Washington State Senate Economic Development and Labor Committee, "A Proposal by Senator Emilio Cantu," Washington Pacific Northwest Export Assistance Center, Seattle, p. 7.

35. Opening statement of Norman Sisisky, chairman, *Increasing Small Business Participation in SBA and EXIMBANK Export Financing Programs*, Hearing before the Subcommittee on Exports, Tax Policy, and Special Problems of the House Committee on Small Business, 102 Cong. 1 sess. (GPO, forthcoming).

36. Interview with Daniel J. Harwood, International Trade Promotion Department, Udenrigs HandelsBanken (a division of Copenhagen Handels-Banken), Copenhagen, December 1989.

37. Bruce Swan, "The Trouble with Export Financing," *The Exporter*, vol. 11 (January 1991), p. 28.

38. Research by First Washington Associates, Ltd., quoted in Martha E. Mangelsdorf, "Unfair Trade," *INC.*, vol. 13 (April 1991), p. 33.

39. Interview with Wolfgang Bongertz, Deutsche Bank, Düsseldorf, November 1990.

40. Harwood, interview, December 1989.

41. Mangelsdorf, "Unfair Trade," p. 33.

42. NASDA, "Introduction and Analysis," pp. 35–37.

43. Mangelsdorf, "Unfair Trade," p. 30.

44. European Commission, "Participation of SMEs," p. 30.

45. William C. Lesch, Abdolreza Eshghi, and Golpira S. Eshghi, "A Review of Export Promotion Programs in the Ten Largest Industrial States," in Cavusgil and Czinkota, *International Perspectives*, p. 34.

46. Seringhaus and Rosson, *Government Export Promotion*, p. 180.

47. Interview with Richard Riley, British Overseas Trade Board, Department of Trade and Industry, London, November 1990.

48. Bert Piest and Henk A. Ritsma, "Export Promotion in the Netherlands," in Cavusgil and Czinkota, *International Perspectives*, pp. 96–97.

49. Riley, interview, November 1990.

50. Interview with Michael Chabrat, MIRCEB, Rennes, Brittany, November 1990.

51. Interview with Norman Arends, MIRCEB, Rennes, Brittany, November 1990.

52. Chabrat, interview, November 1990.

53. Ferdinand Protzman, "Greetings from Fortress Germany," *New York Times*, August 18, 1991, p. 3-1.

54. Charles Batchelor, "A Taste for Cooperation," *Financial Times*, July 24, 1990, p. 10.

55. European Commission, "Participation of SMEs," p. 18.

56. Interview with Philippe Grabli, DML & Associates, Paris, November 1990.

## Notes to Chapter 5

1. Economic Development Corporation of North Rhine-Westphalia, "Products, Diversity, Innovation. . . . Made in Germany," a promotional publication on the NRW economy, 1990.

2. Igor Reichlin, "Sake at the Biergarten: It's 'Tokyo-on-the-Rhine,'" *Business Week*, June 3, 1991, p. 48.

3. For a detailed, though already somewhat outdated, discussion of this concept, see F. H. Rolf Seringhaus and Philip J. Rosson, *Government Export Promotion: A Global Perspective* (Routledge, 1990), pp. 33–45.

4. Interview with Niels Christian Nielsen, Danish Technology Institute, Aarhus, December 1989.

5. Interview with Hans-Wilhelm Dunner, Bundesverband der Selbstandigen, Bonn, November 1990.

6. Graham Bannock and Partners, *Into Active Exporting* (London: British Overseas Trade Board, 1987), p. 26.

7. Interview with Richard Riley, British Overseas Trade Board, Department of Trade and Industry, London, November 1990.

8. Interview with Alain Paupert, Compagnie Francaise d'Assurance pour le Commerce Exterieur, Paris, November 1990.

9. Testimony of Philippe Houchois, former MIRCEB Northwest (U.S.) Office Manager, before the Oregon Joint Trade and Economic Development Commission, February 16, 1990.

10. Interview with Martin F. Parnell, Liverpool Business School, November 1990.

11. Interview with Tell Hermanson, Stockholm Chamber of Commerce, December 1989.

12. Interview with Michele Simonin, Chargee d'Etudes et de Recherche, Chambre de Commerce et d'Industrie de Paris, November 1990.

13. Dunner, interview, November 1990.

14. Joseph Cortright, *Old World New Ideas: Business Assistance Lessons from Europe* (University of Washington, Northwest Policy Center, 1990), p. 7.

15. This is true of most, but not all, Italian manufacturing networks. In some cases, networks are composed of producers of individual components of a complex final product, thus involving firms in several sectors.

16. "Business Is Done by Smaller Companies," a joint publication of the National Industrial Board and the Development Fund, Sweden, n.d., p. 3.

17. Interview with Lars Haggmark, Ministry of Industry, Stockholm, December 1989.

18. Interview with Göran Sjöberg, Swedish Trade Council, Stockholm, December 1989.

19. Interview with Benny Hjern, Swedish Council for Research in the Social Sciences and Humanities, Stockholm, December 1989.

## Notes to Chapter 6

1. Interview with Adele Massi, Istituto Nazionale per il Commercio Estero, Rome, December 1989.

2. Joseph Cortright, *Old World New Ideas: Business Assistance Lessons from Europe* (University of Washington, Northwest Policy Center, 1990), p. 31.

3. Patrizio Bianchi, "Industrial Policy in Italy at a Local Level," cited in Cortright, *Old World New Ideas*, p. 13.

4. "Business Is Done By Smaller Companies," a joint publication of the National Industrial Board and the Development Fund, Sweden, n.d., p. 3.

5. Interview with Norman Arends, MIRCEB, Rennes, Brittany, November 1990.

6. Testimony of Philippe Houchois, former NIRCEB Northwest (U.S.) Office Manager before the Joint Committee on Trade and Economic Development, Oregon Legislative Assembly, February 16, 1990.

7. Interview with Tell Hermanson, Stockholm Chamber of Commerce, December 1989.

8. Interview with Massimo Daolio, RESFOR, Parma, Italy, December 1989.

9. Interview with Mauro Cavagnaro, SVEX S.r.l., Bologna, Italy, December 1989.

10. Interview with Gunter Kayser, Institut fur Mittelstandforschung, Bonn, November 1990.

11. Interview with Howard Gladwell, Department of Trade and Industry, Birmingham, November 1990.

12. Interview with Jean-Claude Moyon, Foreign Trade Department, Chamber of Commerce and Industry, Rennes, France, November 1990.

13. Interview with Helga Massow, Foreign Trade Promotion Institute, North Rhine-Westphalia, November 1990.

14. Interview with Niels Christian Nielsen, Danish Technology Institute, Aarhus, 1989.

15. British Overseas Trade Board, *Forward Plan* (London: Department of Trade and Industry, 1990), p. 33.

## Notes to Chapter 7

1. James McNiven, *Challenge and Response: The Rise of State Export Development Policies in the U.S.* (Halifax, Nova Scotia: Dalhousie University Centre for International Business Studies, April 1989), p. 11.

2. William Krist, American Electronics Association, *Export Trade Promotion Programs, Federal and Private Sector Roles*, Hearing before the Subcommittee on International Economic Policy and Trade of the House Committee on Foreign Affairs, 101 Cong. 2 sess. (Government Printing Office, 1991).

3. Susan C. Schwab, "Building a National Export Development Alliance," *Intergovernmental Perspectives*, vol. 16 (Spring 1990), p. 19.

4. U.S. General Accounting Office, National Security and International Affairs Division, *Export Promotion: Federal Programs Lack Organization and Funding Cohesiveness* (Washington, January 1992), p. 1.

5. This is still the case in several states, especially in the South.

6. National Association of State Development Agencies (NASDA), "Introduction and Analysis of 1990 SEPD Data," Washington, 1991, p. 18.

7. Robert Thomas Kudrie and Cynthia Marie Kite, "The Evaluation of State Programs for International Business Development," *Economic Development Quarterly*, vol. 3 (November 1989), p.289.

8. NASDA, "Introduction and Analysis," p. 14.

9. Tommy G. Thompson, "Going Global: A Governor's Perspective," *Intergovernmental Perspective*, vol. 16 (Spring 1990), p. 15.

10. NASDA, "Introduction and Analysis," p. 45.

11. Blaine Liner, "States and Localities in the Global Marketplace," *Intergovernmental Perspective*, vol. 16 (Spring 1990), p. 11.

12. NASDA, "Introduction and Analysis," p. 37.

13. Michigan Department of Commerce, "Trends in State Export Promotion Strategies," Lansing, 1989.

14. Liner, "States and Localities," p. 14.

15. Carol Conway, "State International Budget Trends," *Clearinghouse on State International Policies*, newsletter of the Southern International Policy Network, Southern Growth Policies Board and the Economic Development Administration, vol. 1, May 1991, p. 3.

16. Kudrie and Kite, "Evaluation of State Programs," p. 289.

17. Charles Cadwell, *State Export Promotion and Small Business* (Washington: U.S. Small Business Administration, 1992), p. iv.

18. S. Tamer Cavusgil, "Export Development Efforts in the United States: Experiences and Lessons Learned," in *International Perspectives on Trade Promotion and Assistance*, S. Tamer Cavusgil and Michael R. Czinkota, eds. (New York: Quorum Books, 1990), pp. 176–78.

19. For a more extensive review of similarities and differences, see Joseph Cortright, *Old World New Ideas: Business Assistance Lessons from Europe* (University of Washington, Northwest Policy Center, 1990), pp. 31–35.

20. Representative Andy Ireland, *Increasing Small Business Participation in SBA and EXIMbank Financing Programs*, Hearing before the Subcommittee on Exports, Tax Policy, and Special Problems of the House Committee on Small Business, 102 Cong. 1 sess. (Government Printing Office, 1991).

21. Dun and Bradstreet Corporation, "Prospects for Exporters in 1991-92: The Dun's 5,000 Export Survey," *Dun and Bradstreet Comments on the Economy*, vol. 2 (August–September 1991), p. 1.

22. Dun and Bradstreet Corporation, "Prospects for Exporters," pp. 1–4.

# Index

113

Pre-Market Diagnosis program (Denmark), 26–27
Private and quasi-private providers of export assistance, 67–72; chambers of commerce, 68–69, 72–74, 89

Quality Management System (U.K.), 44, 87

Reagan administration, 88
Real services, provision of, 82
Regional Assistance and Consultancy Fund (FRAC) (France), 45
Regional Development Funds (RDFs) (Sweden), 26, 32, 75, 77–78
Regional Mission for the Coordination of International Trade with Brittany (MIRCEB), 39, 60–62, 64, 71, 82
Regional targeting of export assistance, 74–78, 95–96
RESFOR, 12, 60, 75–76, 84
Ricotta, Enrico, 22, 57
Riley, Richard, 83

Schwab, Susan, 88–89
Sectoral targeting of export assistance, 74–78, 95–96
Service card system, 87
Service Center for the Export Development of Emilia-Romagna Firms (SVEX), 36–37, 60, 64, 84
Simonin, Michele, 18
Simpler Trade Procedures (SITPRO) Board (U.K.), 53
Sisisky, Norman, 55
Sjöberg, Göran, 18, 28, 78
Small- and medium-sized firms (SMEs): close to home trading, 39–40; defining characteristics, 27–28; export-ready firms, 22–28; export-willing firms, 28–37, 96–97; as focus of export assistance efforts, 10–11, 23; strategic exporting, failure to engage in, 17–19; in United States, 8–9

Small Business Administration (U.S.), 9, 55–56, 91
Small Business Association of New England, 13
Solberg, Carl Arthur, 49
Spain, 3
Stahl, Willy, 46
Strategic exporting, 10; programs on, 19–21; small firms' failure to engage in, 17–19
Stroh, Leslie, 8–9
Subsidies, 80, 82
SVEX, 36–37, 60, 64, 84
Sweden: chambers of commerce, 73; close to home trading, 39–40; customization of export assistance programs, 60; export assistance financing, 82, 83–84, 85; export audit programs, 26; export orientation, 2; private/public status of export assistance providers, 68; regional and sectoral targeting of export assistance, 75, 77–78; small- and medium-sized firms, definition of, 27; training programs for company staff, 30–33; transactional services, 52–53
Swedish Trade Council, 18, 30, 31, 32, 52–53, 60, 75, 77, 82, 85
Switzerland, 3

Taupin, Fabrice, 54
Touzé, Olivier, 54
Trade and Industry Department (U.K.), 17, 68, 81–82, 84, 86
Trade development programs, 62–65
Trade fairs: government sponsorship of, 47–48; private sponsorship of, 48–49; pros and cons of, 49–51
Trade Opportunities Program (U.S.), 42
Trading companies, 34–35
Training programs for company staff, 29–31; program profiles, 31–34

Transactional barriers, 51–52
Transactional services, 52–54

United Kingdom, 1; chambers of commerce, 68–69, 73; close to home
trading, 39; competitiveness strategy, 98; customization of export assistance programs, 58, 59; export assistance financing, 80, 81–82, 86–
87; export audit programs, 24–25;
export barriers, 15–16; export orientation, 3; intelligence-gathering services, 42–44; market exposure programs, 48, 50; private/public status
of export assistance providers, 68–
69, 71; regional and sectoral targeting of export assistance, 75; training programs for company staff, 30;
transactional services, 53
United States: chambers of commerce,
72, 73, 89; competitiveness of companies, 6; competitiveness strategy,
need for, 98–99; concern about export growth, need for, 94–95; customization of export assistance programs, 58, 59–60; European export
assistance programs, adaptation of,
92–93; export barriers, perceptions

of, 12–14; export financing, 55–57;
export infrastructure, inadequacy of,
88–89; export market development,
shortcomings in, 97; export patterns, 7–8; export promotion, 4–5,
97; export "turnaround" of 1990s,
5–6, 101n10; future outlook for exporting, 99–100; guiding principles
for export assistance program, 94–
99; intelligence-gathering services,
42; market exposure programs, 50;
"pep talk" approach to export assistance, 9; small- and medium-sized
firms, export potential of, 8–9, 96;
state trade programs, 89–92; trade
deficit, 5, 6; training programs for
company staff, 29, 30
Urban Institute (U.S.), 91, 92
U.S. and Foreign Commercial Service
(US&FCS), 42, 88–89, 91

Vogt, Victor, 14

Wengler, Stefan, 19

XPORT trading company, 59–60

Yankelovich, Skelly, and White, 13